MW01671166

F04 Pinnacle Club

Congratulations!

[illegible]

JACKSON HOLE

CROSSROADS *of the* WEST

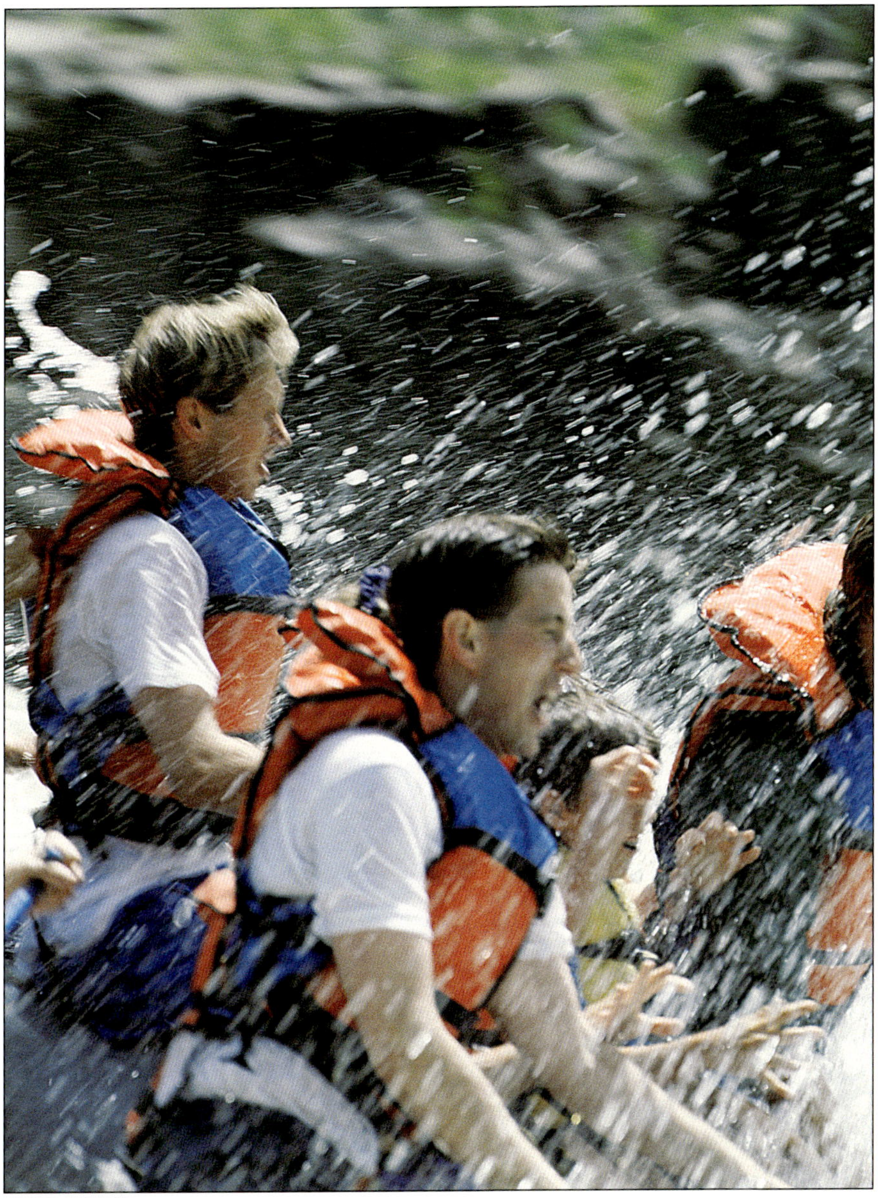

LELAND HOWARD

by Connie Wieneke

AMERICAN & WORLD GEOGRAPHIC PUBLISHING

For Richard,
whose desire brought us here.

LELAND HOWARD

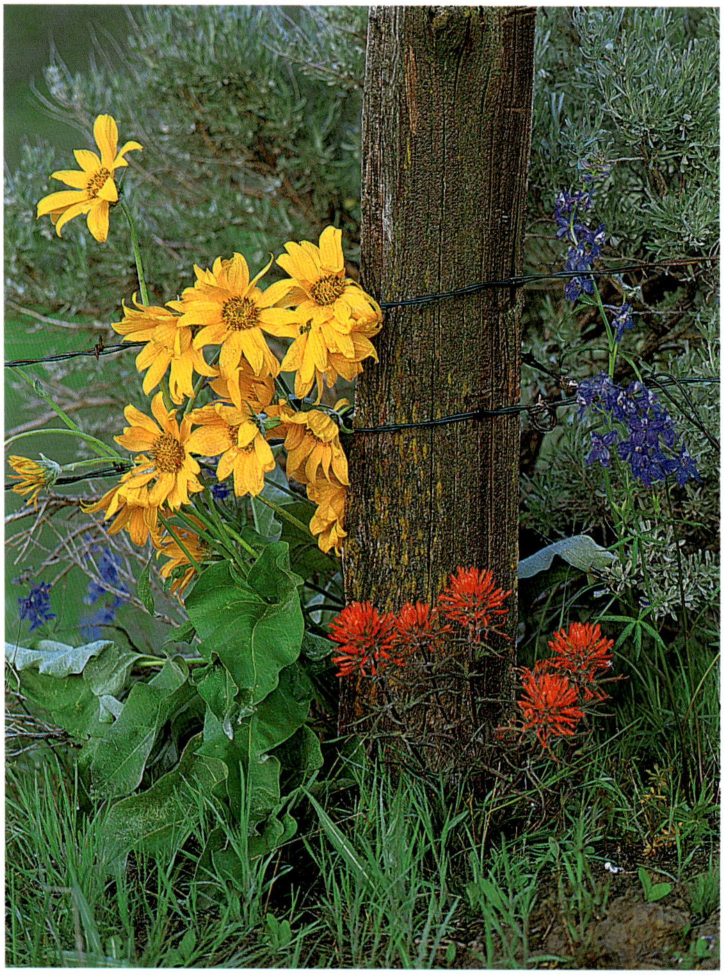

Jackson Hole wildflowers have short seasons in which to flaunt their stuff.

Title page: Whitewater rafting on the Snake River.

Front cover: Moose cow and twin calves at sunrise along the Snake River in Grand Teton National Park. DIANA STRATTON

Back cover: The town of Jackson viewed from Snow King Mountain. DIANA STRATTON

Write for our catalog:
American & World Geographic Publishing, P.O. Box 5630, Helena, MT 59604.

GLENN VAN NIMWEGEN

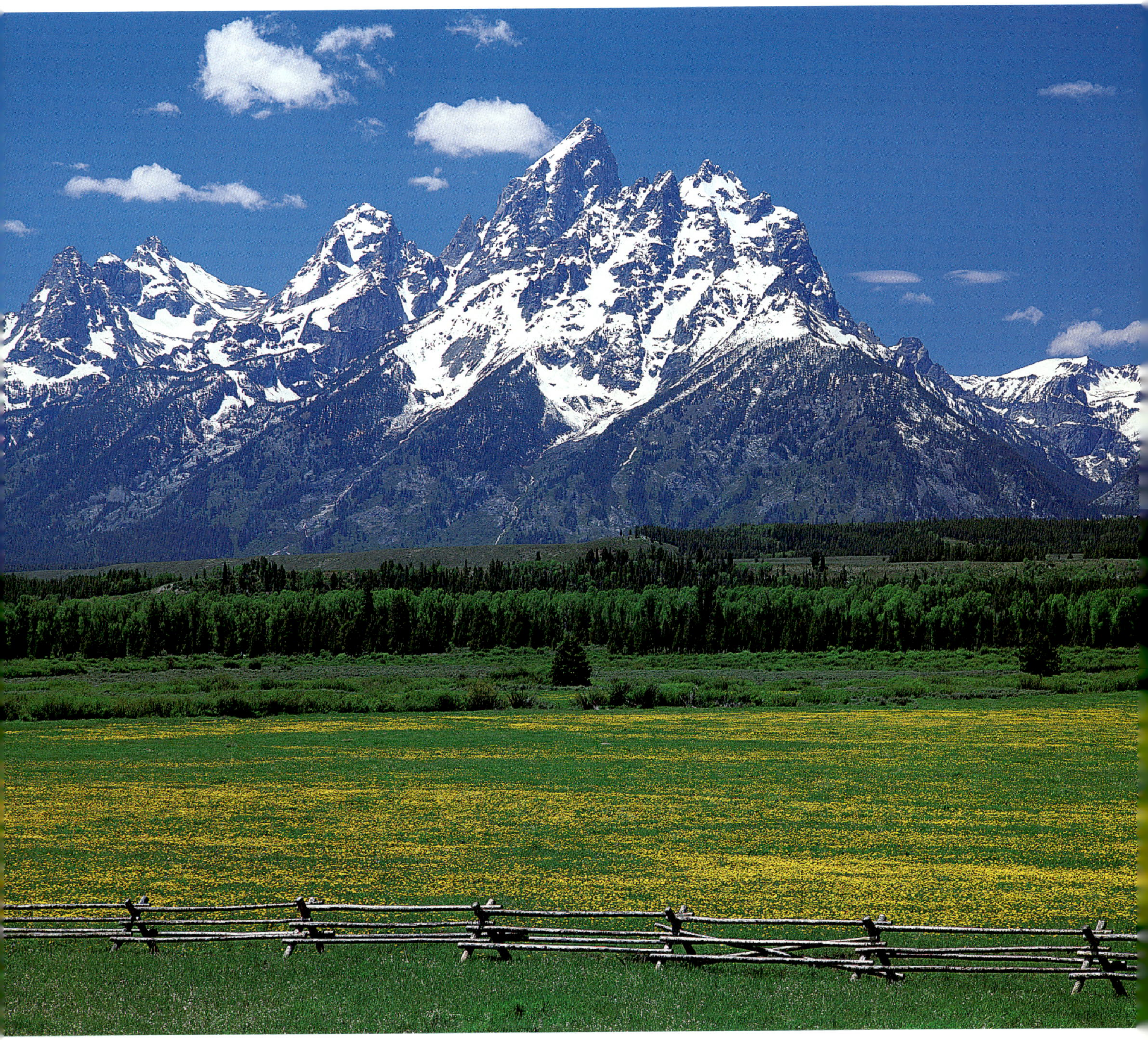

The Grand Teton thrusts its awesome bulk to the sky over the placid, dandelion-bedecked plain.

Connie Wieneke has been an active resident of Jackson Hole since 1983. Reared in Seattle, she is a University of Washington graduate and has an MFA from the University of Montana where she studied writing with William Kittredge. Wieneke was a newspaper editor and reporter in Washington and Wyoming for twelve years. She has published one other book, an art monograph for the Wyoming State Museum, and has published fiction, essays, and poetry. She skis, bicycles and backpacks in her spare time from a home in Wilson that she shares with her husband, eight chickens and two frogs.

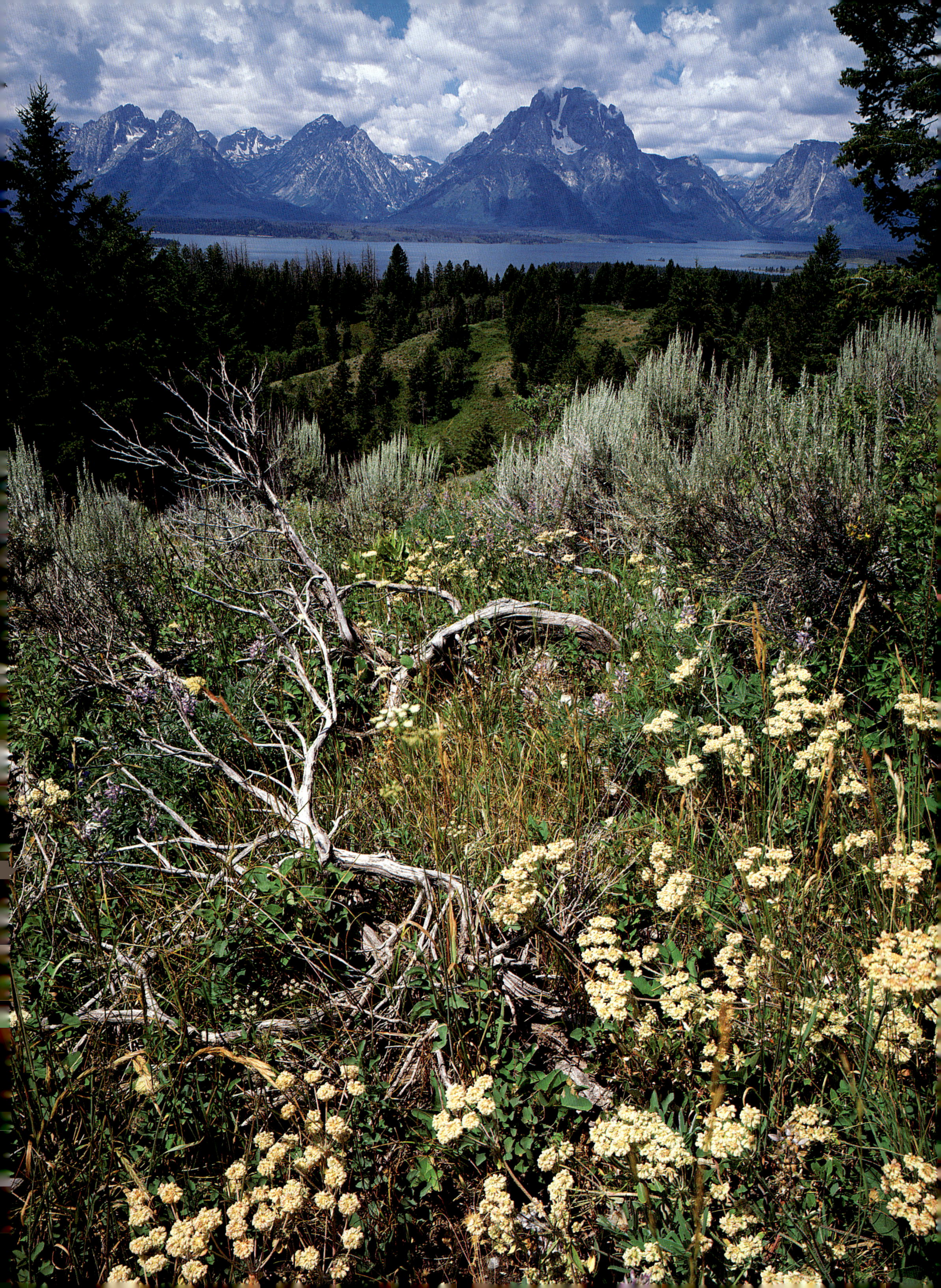

DIANA STRATTON

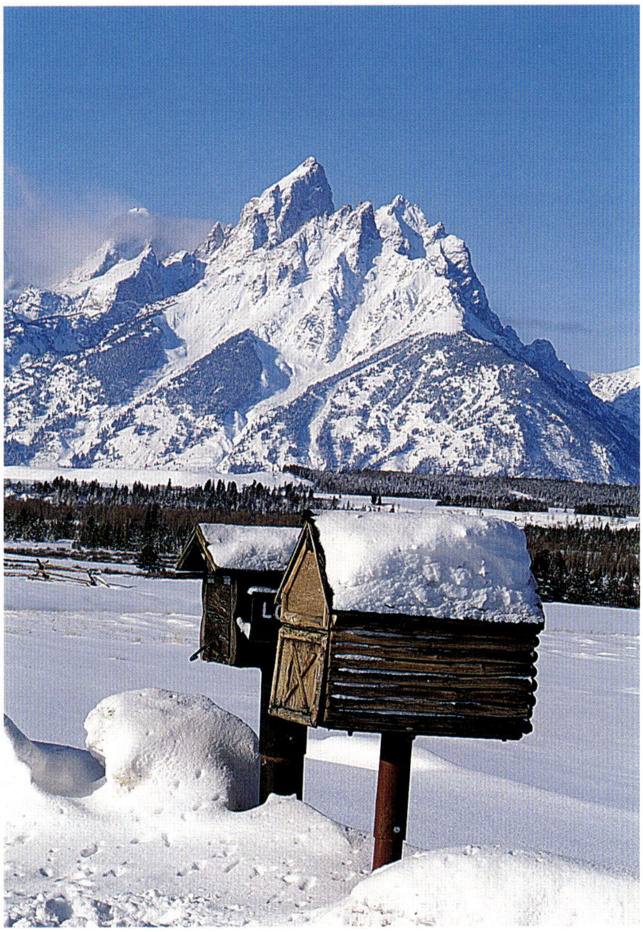

CONTENTS

Above: Mailboxes reflect the rustic western look of Jackson Hole architecture.

Facing page: The Teton Range viewed from a patch of wildflowers on Signal Mountain in Grand Teton National Park. CHARLIE BORLAND

Overleaf: Mount Moran dominates a view of Jackson Lake in Grand Teton National Park. RUSS FINLEY/ BORLAND STOCK PHOTO

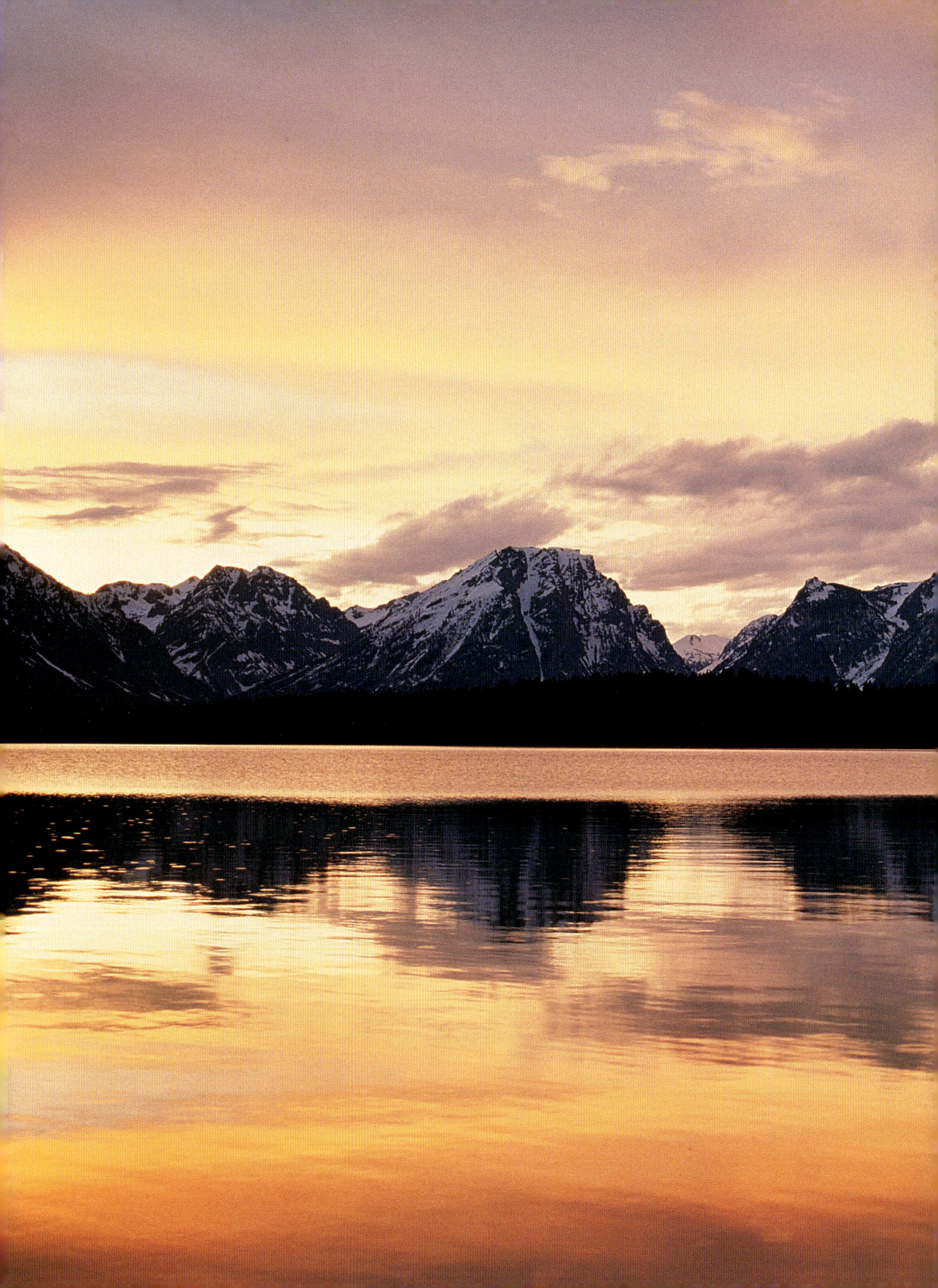

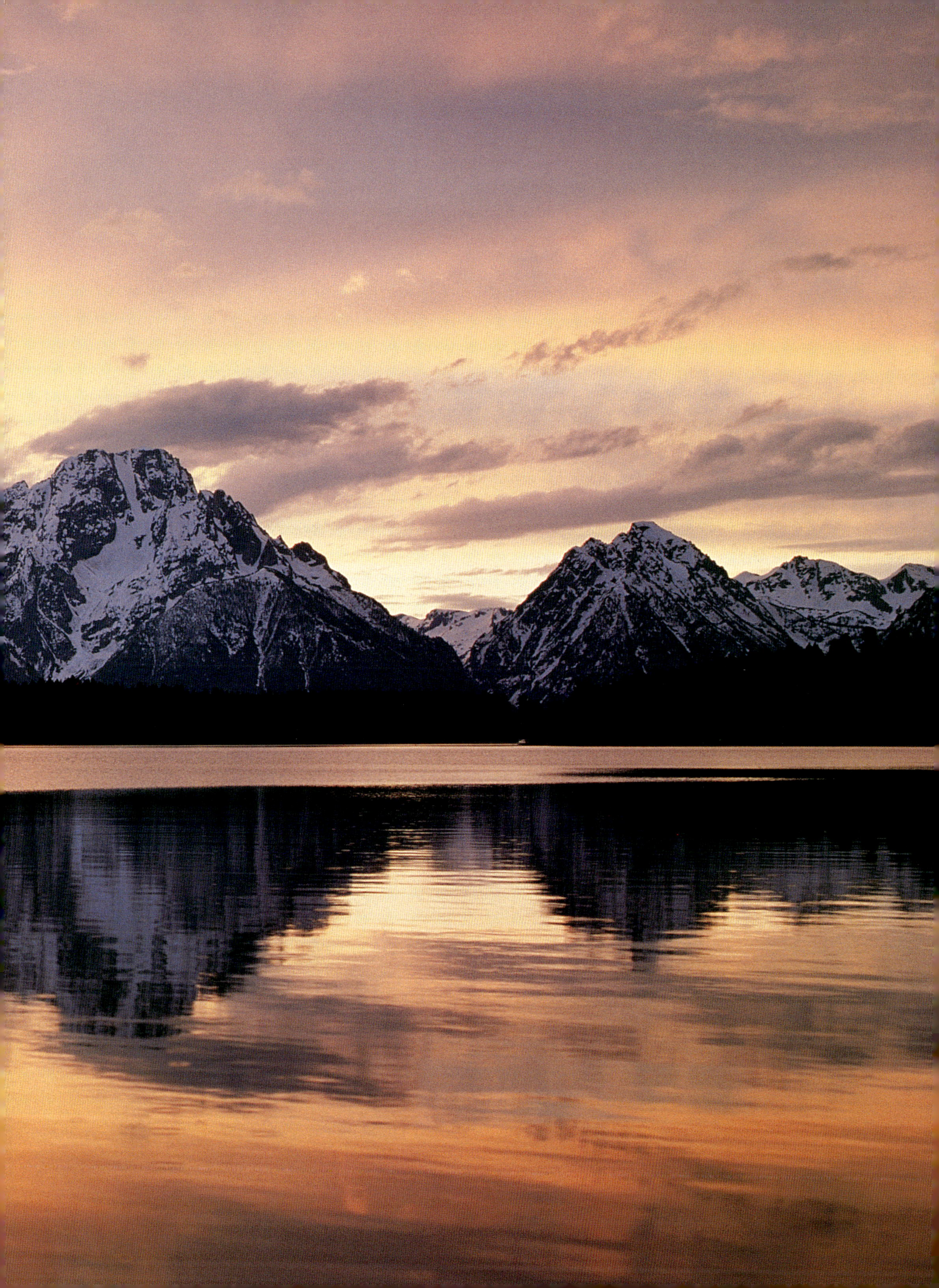

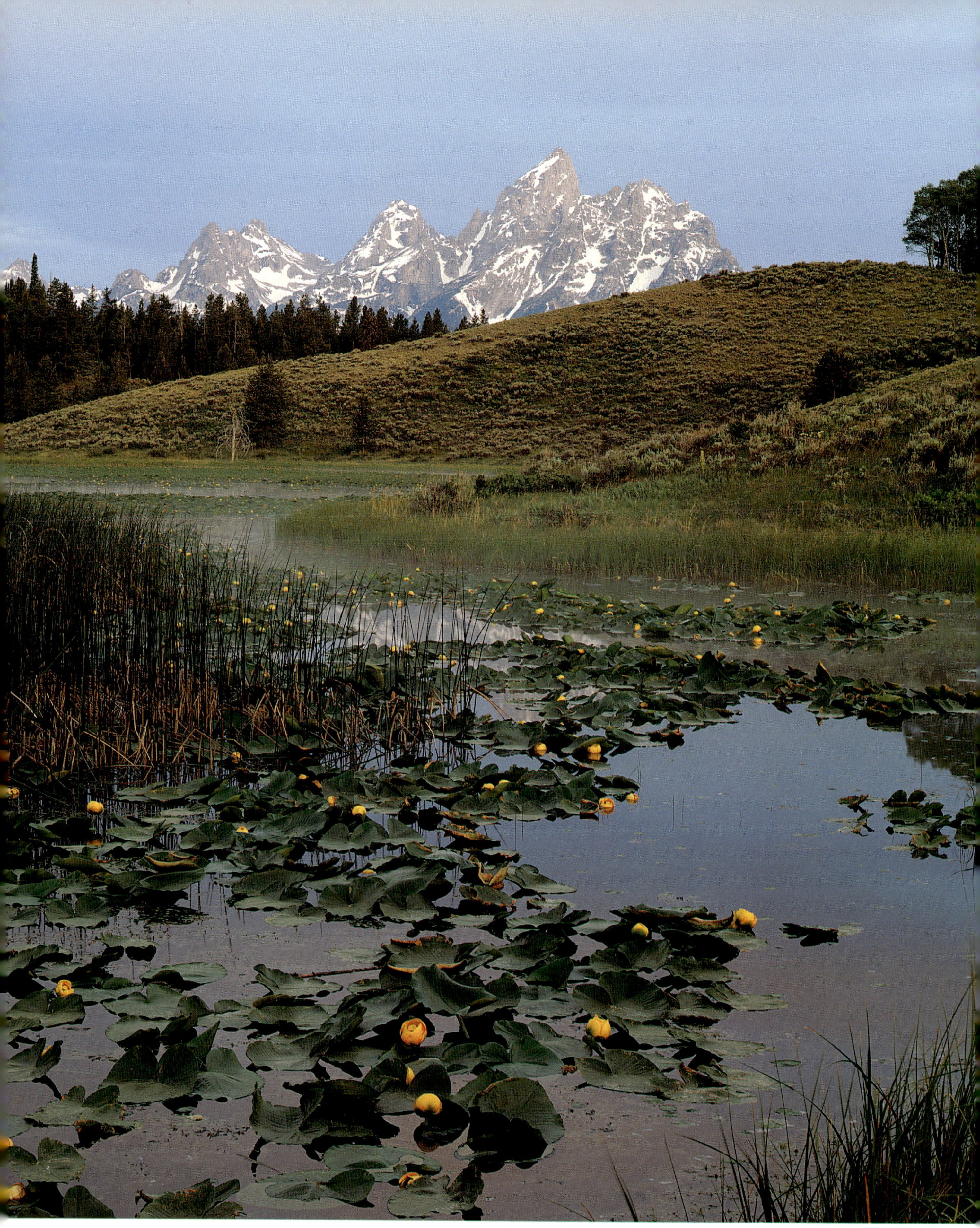

Yellow, or Indian, pondlilies in Grand Teton National Park greet a sunrise reflecting from the Teton Range.
GLENN VAN NIMWEGEN

HENRY H. HOLDSWORTH

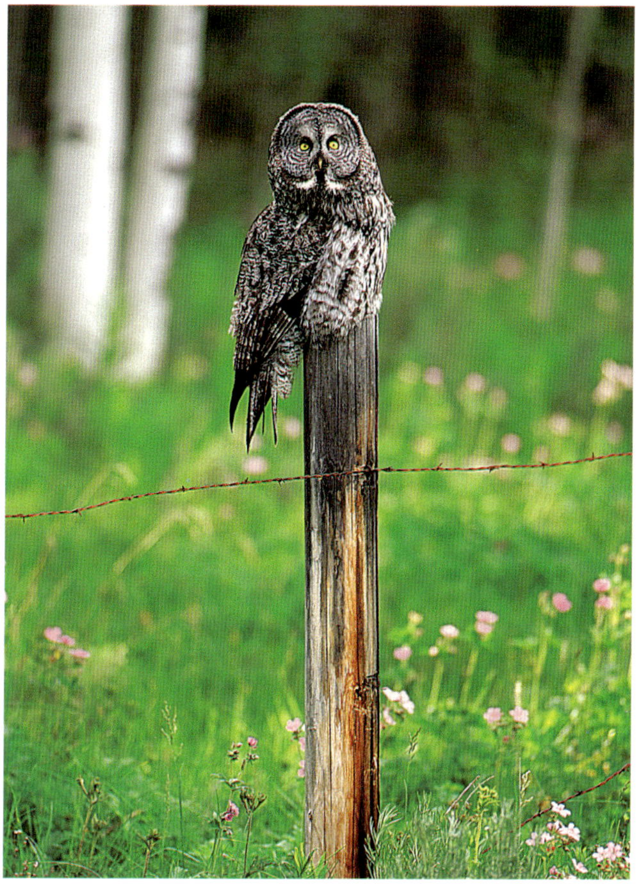

Left: Great gray owl surveys terrain that includes scattering of sticky geraniums.

Below: Weathered barn and weathered bike in Jackson Hole.

ESTHER E. THOMPSON

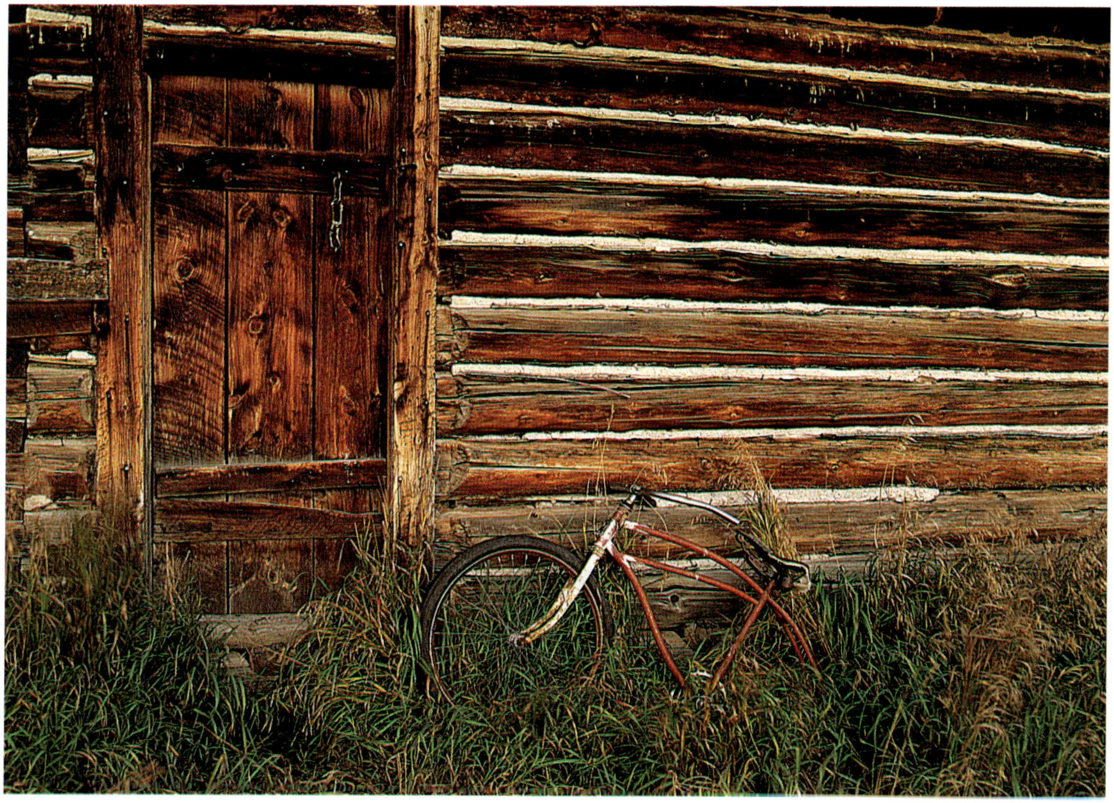

DEBI OTTINGER

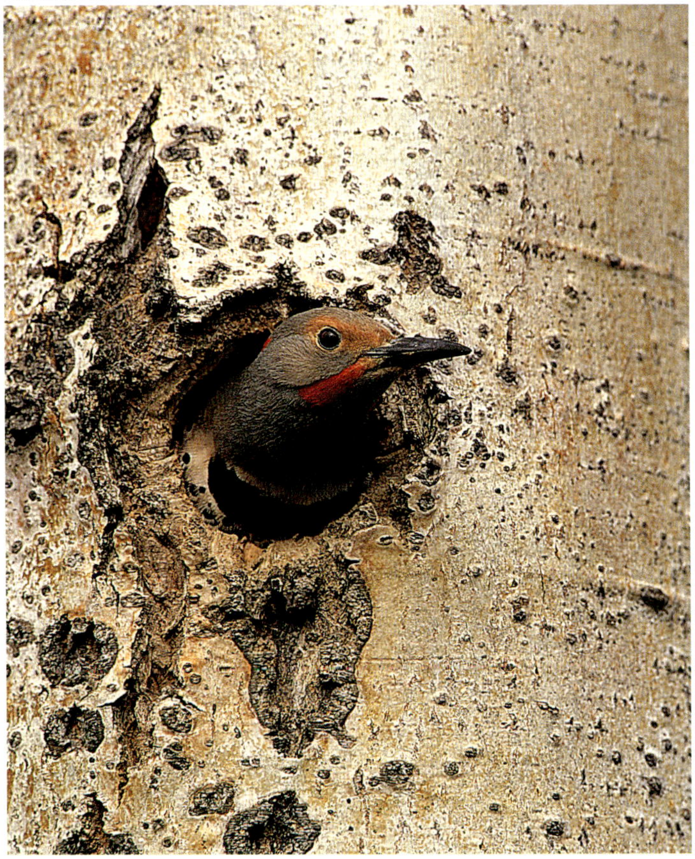

Right: A male northern flicker checks out the landscape from his nesting hole near Jackson.

Below: Jackson Hole and Grand Teton National Park provide world-class fishing in crystalline streams.

Facing page: Kayakers' quest for thrills in the Snake River Canyon continues in the fall.
DIANA STRATTON

MICHAEL S. QUINTON

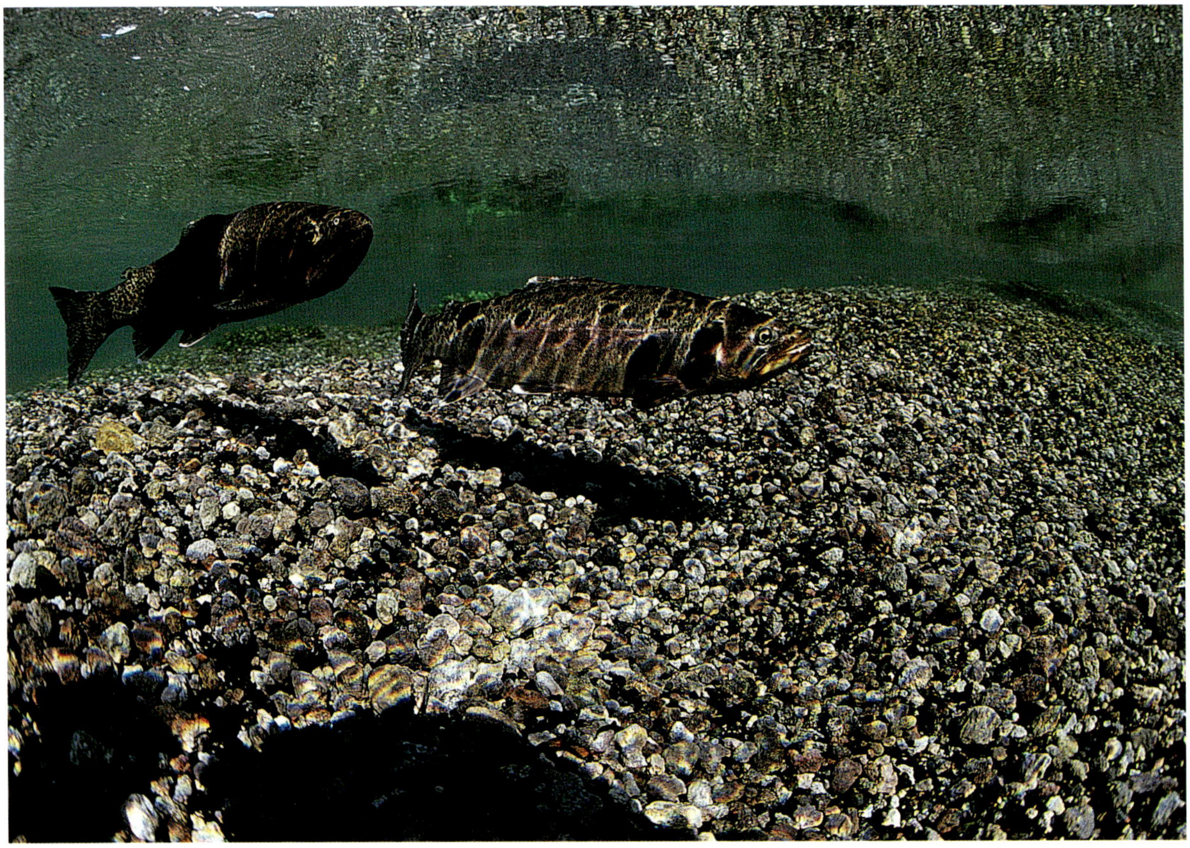

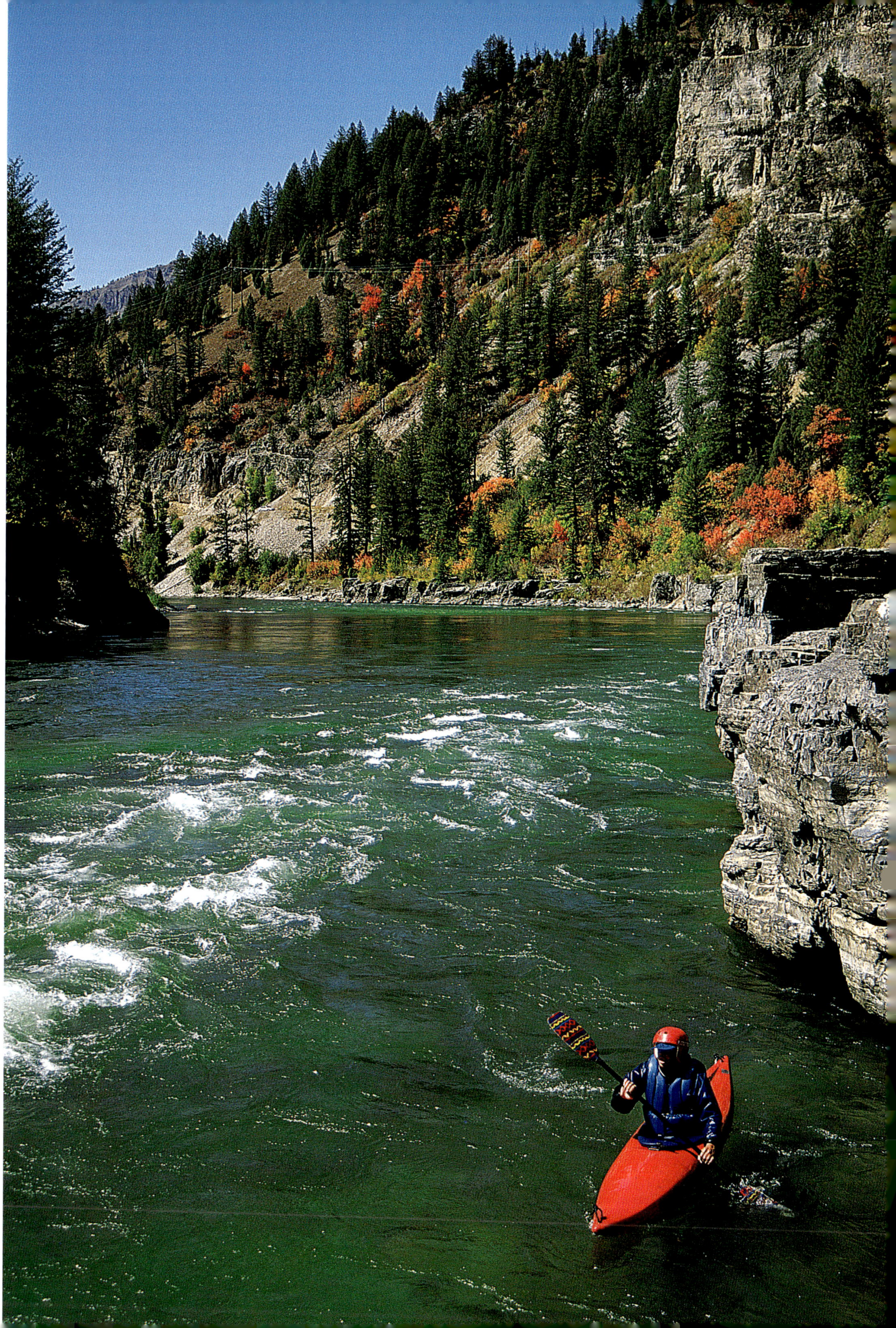

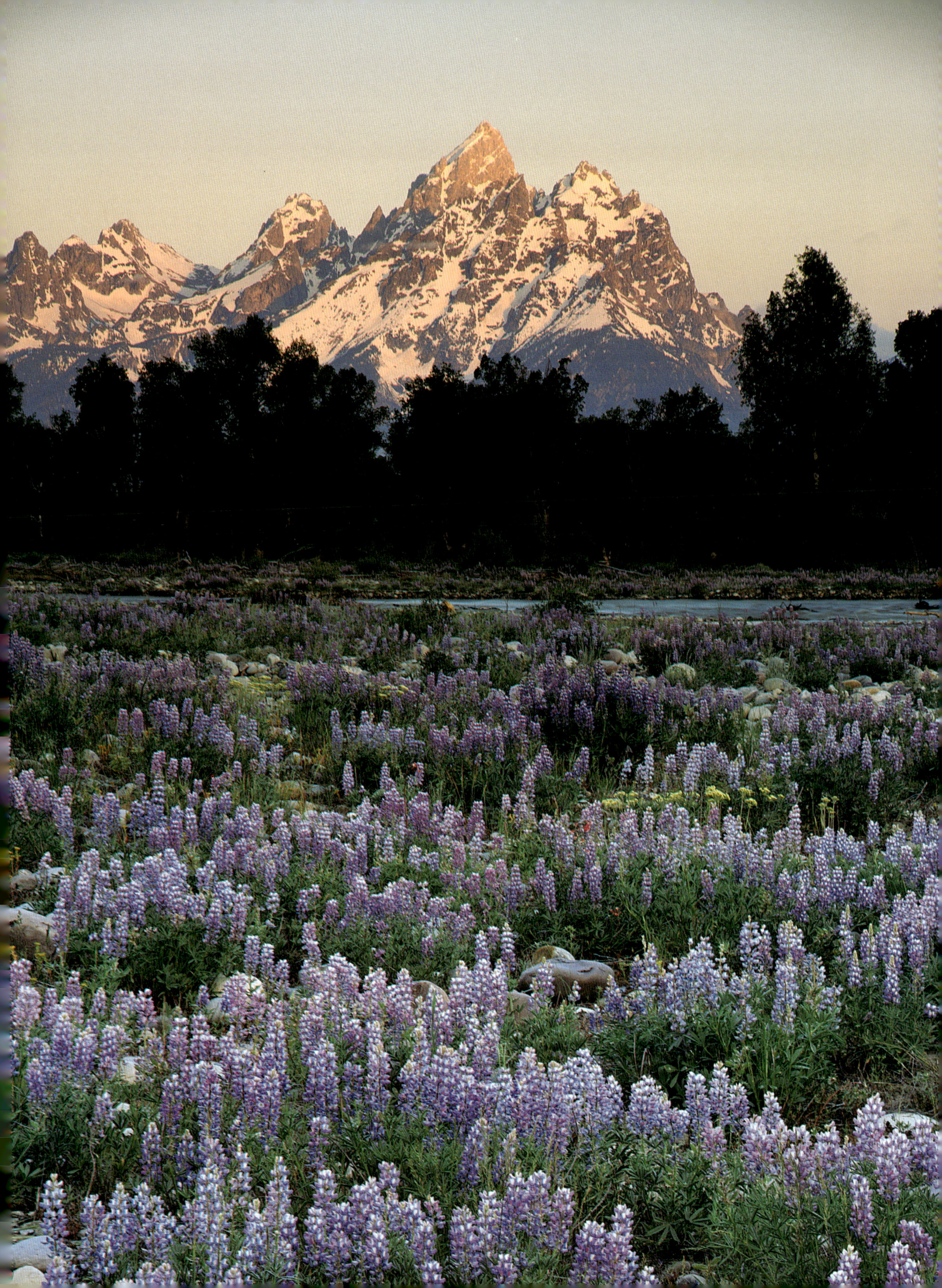

CHAPTER ONE

THE PLACE

The Tetons, forged in a series of globe-shaping events over hundreds of millions of years, jump flat-footed from the plains–whoosh–directly into the sky. No warm-up; no gentle, rounded little foothills gradually elevate the eye. Suddenly, monumentally, there they are–rock pinnacles two miles higher than sea level.

The exposed ridges and spires of the Tetons, made up largely of rock known as gneisses and schists, were formed under great pressure during the Precambrian period, 2 billion years ago. The 300-million-year-long Paleozoic period followed, when a series of ancient seas lapped up onto beaches, leaving behind layers of sandstone, shale and limestone, some of which contains fossilized creatures. How else explain tiny corals, crinoids and mollusks cast in rock above 9,000 feet on Rendezvous Peak, Sleeping Indian, and Fossil Mountain?

What became Jackson Hole remained relatively placid, geologically speaking, until the Paleocene period 65 million years ago when volcanic fireworks in Yellowstone began pummeling the area. In the Miocene period, a mere 25 million years ago, volcanoes erupted and lava flowed in the as-yet-to-be-formed valley. The most dramatic event, however, was set in motion only 9 million years ago: the block of metamorphic rock that would become the Tetons started its incremental shift upward in the west, while what would become the Hole sank slowly, foot-by-foot, to the east. That process continues today.

Beginning 200,000 years ago, three waves of glaciers buried Jackson Hole beneath 1,000 to 2,000 feet of ice. On their advances and retreats, massive glaciers scoured rock and soil, gouged canyons out of granite and scattered moraines in their wake. The human mind reels to picture Signal Mountain near Moran or Blacktail Butte near Moose covered by a sea of ice as recently as 15,000 years ago. The cirques and hanging canyons visible from trails and roads speak tellingly of these periods of glaciation. The melting glaciers also left a legacy at the toe of the Tetons: exquisite lakes, such as Leigh and Jenny, Bradley and Phelps, to mirror the mountains. Reminding us of those icy epochs are a half dozen glaciers; the largest is the receding Teton Glacier, cupped between the Grand and Mount Owen.

In the mountains, weather cannot be avoided. We can only protect ourselves against it or make the most of it. Think of the mountains and you'll be thinking Weather with a capital "W." A number of sayings circulate about our local weather, the most telling

Facing page: Sunrise spotlights Grand Teton. GLENN VAN NIMWEGEN

being, "There are only two seasons in Jackson Hole: Winter and July." All of that translates into snow any day of the year, cool nights for sleeping in mid-summer, and temperature swings of as much as 50 degrees in a single day. For the serious gardener such weather means battling to grow tomatoes and squash in a place with barely a month of frost-free mornings.

"We're in a combination of climates here," explained meteorologist Jim Woodmency. "There's an alpine zone running through the mountains; then we've got semiarid conditions running in the valley." Such topography means Jackson averages 82 inches of snow annually, while at 9,000 feet, between 400 and 500 inches are recorded during the same period. For skiers, this translates into a bonanza of powder in the heart of winter and a freeway of corn snow in the spring. It also brings with it occasional winter inversions: getting on the tram at the Jackson Hole Ski Area in sub-zero conditions, disembarking minutes later at the top of Rendezvous Bowl with the temperature in the balmy thirties. A good reason to head for the higher slopes.

DIANA STRATTON

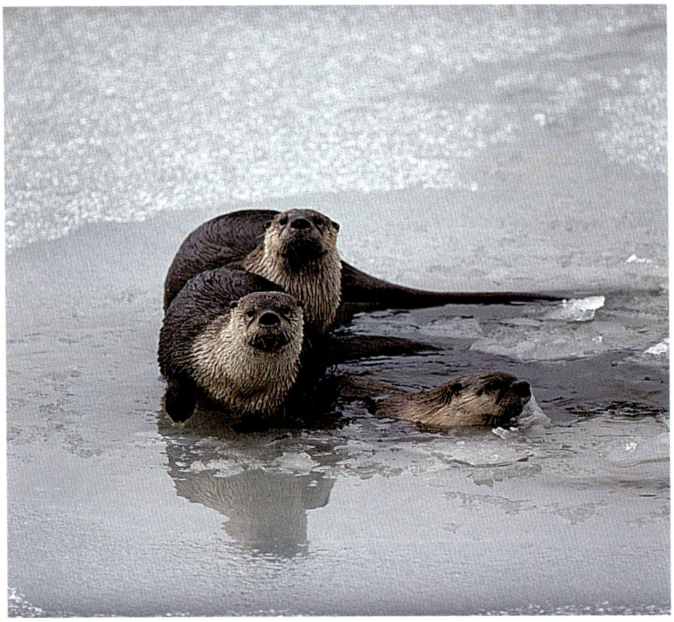

Above: A trio of river otters take a chilly romp in the Snake River.

Facing page: Nature paints a fantasy in fog and frost.
GLENN VAN NIMWEGEN

Many forms of weather come our way, from the run-of-the-mill sprinkle and morning fog to run-for-your-life "microbursts." Severe storms have moved through Jackson Hole over the years, the most devastating of which occurred in 1987 when a microburst mowed down a twenty-mile swath of conifers in the Teton Wilderness.

Oldtimers and newcomers remember weather's extremes: winters when there was too much or too little snow; summers when it rained every day or when it felt like the world would burn up. Although the fires of 1988 in Yellowstone captured the world's attention, Jackson Hole also was threatened by blazes in the nearby forest, the sun rising each day red and apocalyptic.

Snow in the mountains means more than just great skiing; it means water the following summer. Water for irrigating hay and grainfields, for spawning fish, for drinking, for boating whitewater rapids. For reflecting. And not only for the benefit of us in Jackson Hole, but for people dependent on the same resource, from Wyoming through Idaho and on into the Pacific Ocean. What happens in the Tetons and Gros Ventres, the Absarokas and the Snake River Range has consequences beyond our rivers and mountains.

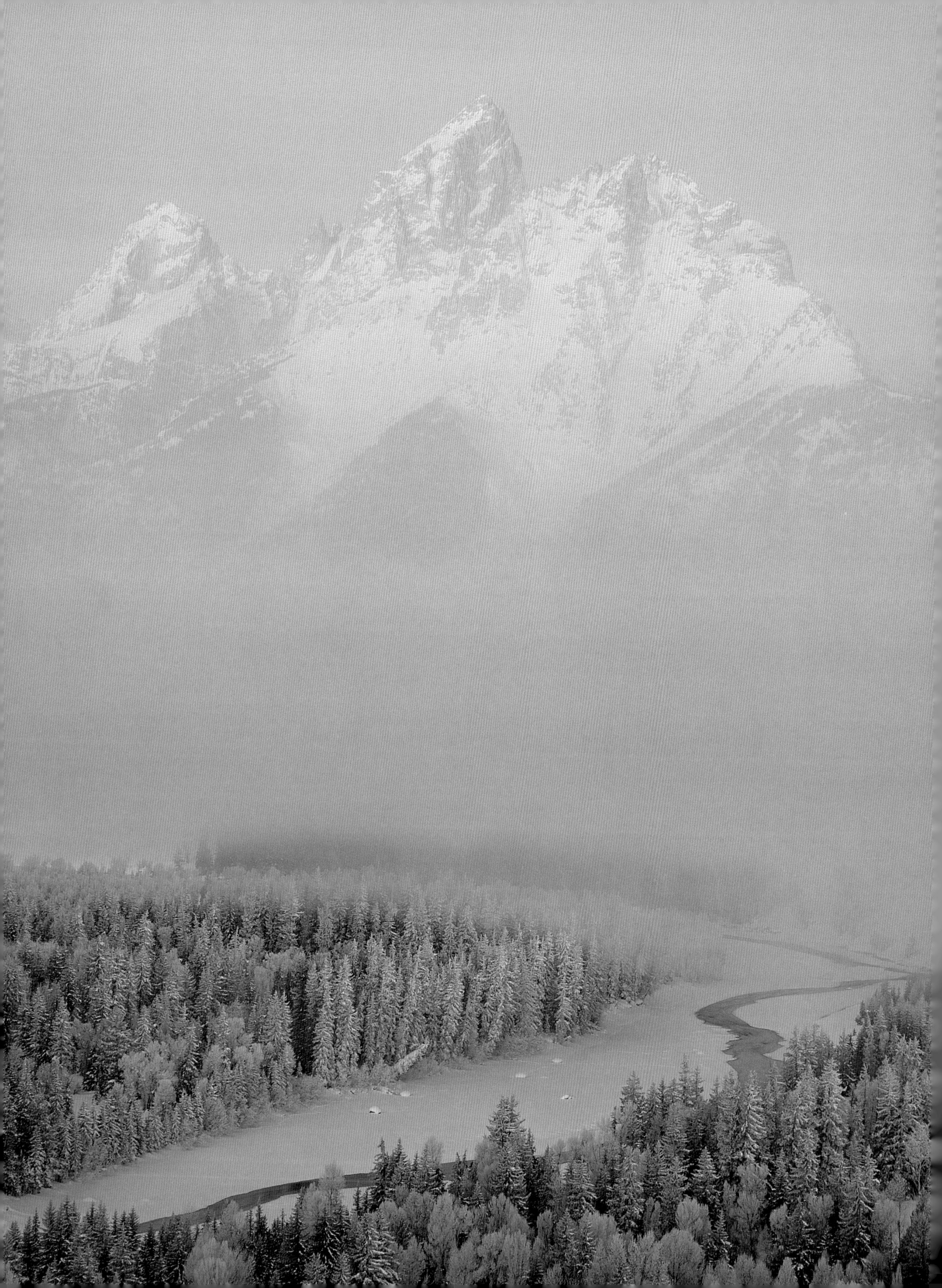

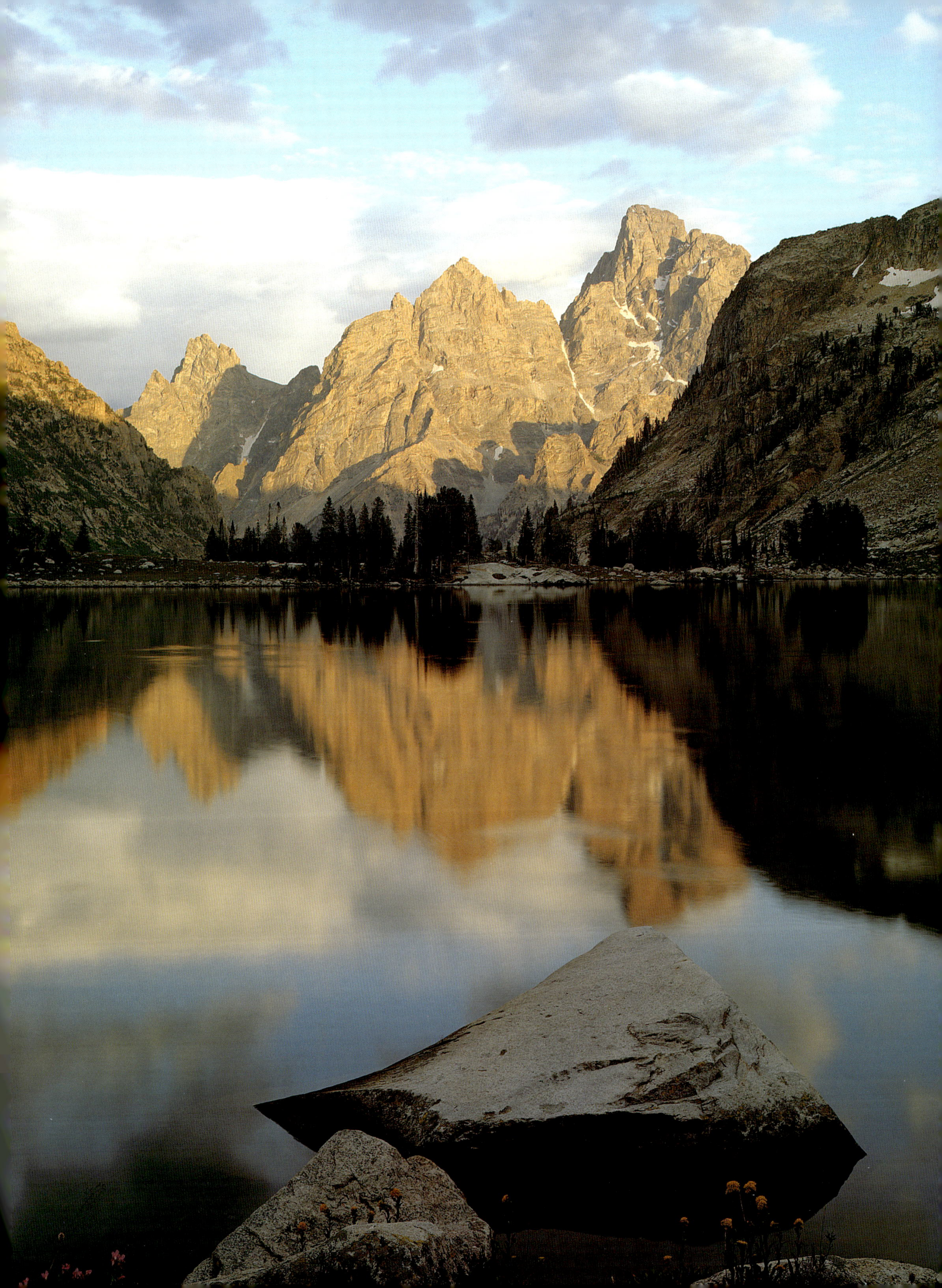

The Continental Divide forms the easternmost rim of Jackson Hole. If we follow the Buffalo Fork toward Marston Pass, Black Rock Creek to Togwotee Pass, or the tributaries of the Gros Ventre River toward Sheridan or Union passes, we will eventually straddle the Continental Divide. From these passes, we could drop into the Wind and Shoshone rivers and make our way into central Wyoming. Via these streams, with portages, we could navigate the Big Horn, Yellowstone, Missouri, and Mississippi rivers to the Atlantic. Not far from Union Pass lies Triple Divide Peak, a geographic point of interest because rain or snow that falls on its slopes ends up in three different seas: the Gulf of Mexico to the southeast, the Gulf of California to the southwest, or the Pacific Ocean to the west.

Ribbons of water connect Jackson Hole to the world. These ribbons begin with the headwaters of the Snake River, with springs, and melting glaciers and snowfields in the mountains that ring us. A close examination of a topographical map reveals the numerous fingers of water that feed into the Snake River from north to south. Tracing their courses, I have sympathized with the early explorers' and fur trappers' confusion when faced with such complex drainages and ridges.

Beginning in the north and flowing into the Snake from the east are, among others, Pacific Creek, the Buffalo Fork, Spread Creek, the Gros Ventre River, Flat Creek, and Horse Creek. Fewer major streams enter the Snake on the west bank, but include Polecat Creek, Granite Creek, Fish Creek and Mosquito Creek. The Hoback River brings water out of the Gros Ventre Mountains and the Wyoming Range, and delineates the southern boundary of Jackson Hole.

Because of the final damming of Jackson Lake in 1917 and the presence of levees on its main channel, the Snake River no longer takes a serpentine course through the valley. Levees on the Buffalo Fork, Black Rock Creek, and the Gros Ventre and Hoback rivers also were completed by the early 1960s. The long-term effects of such control of nature on the native flora, fauna, and soil have not been adequately studied. But those of us living in the flood plain near Wilson are grateful for the levees.

The natural course of the Snake River was diverted by homesteaders into ditches for irrigating hayfields; now these ditches are tapped as well to water golf courses and to fill reflecting ponds in subdivisions. Smaller rivers and streams also were changed to suit agricultural purposes during the first decades of this century, with irrigation dams constructed by ranchers on Spread Creek and the Gros Ventre. Soon after Cache Creek escapes from the canyon directly east of Jackson, it disappears for long stretches beneath downtown streets and buildings. Listen, and you will hear it humming along the sidewalks of Broadway and Deloney.

More of Jackson Hole's water might have been exploited if not for the vigilance of early settlers and dude ranchers. In the 1920s, plans by outsiders to dam Jenny and Leigh lakes to provide water for Idaho farmers were squelched. Today's residents and visitors are grateful for their watchfulness, welcoming the wild aspects of the Snake and other valley streams, preferring to fly fish and run rapids.

Sometimes nature, without a by-your-leave, has controlled water and the land in its own way. In May 1925, more than 20,000 cubic yards of rock and mud separated itself

Facing page: Lake Solitude, in the backcountry of Grand Teton National Park, provides a different perspective on Grand Teton. GLENN VAN NIMWEGEN

HENRY H. HOLDSWORTH

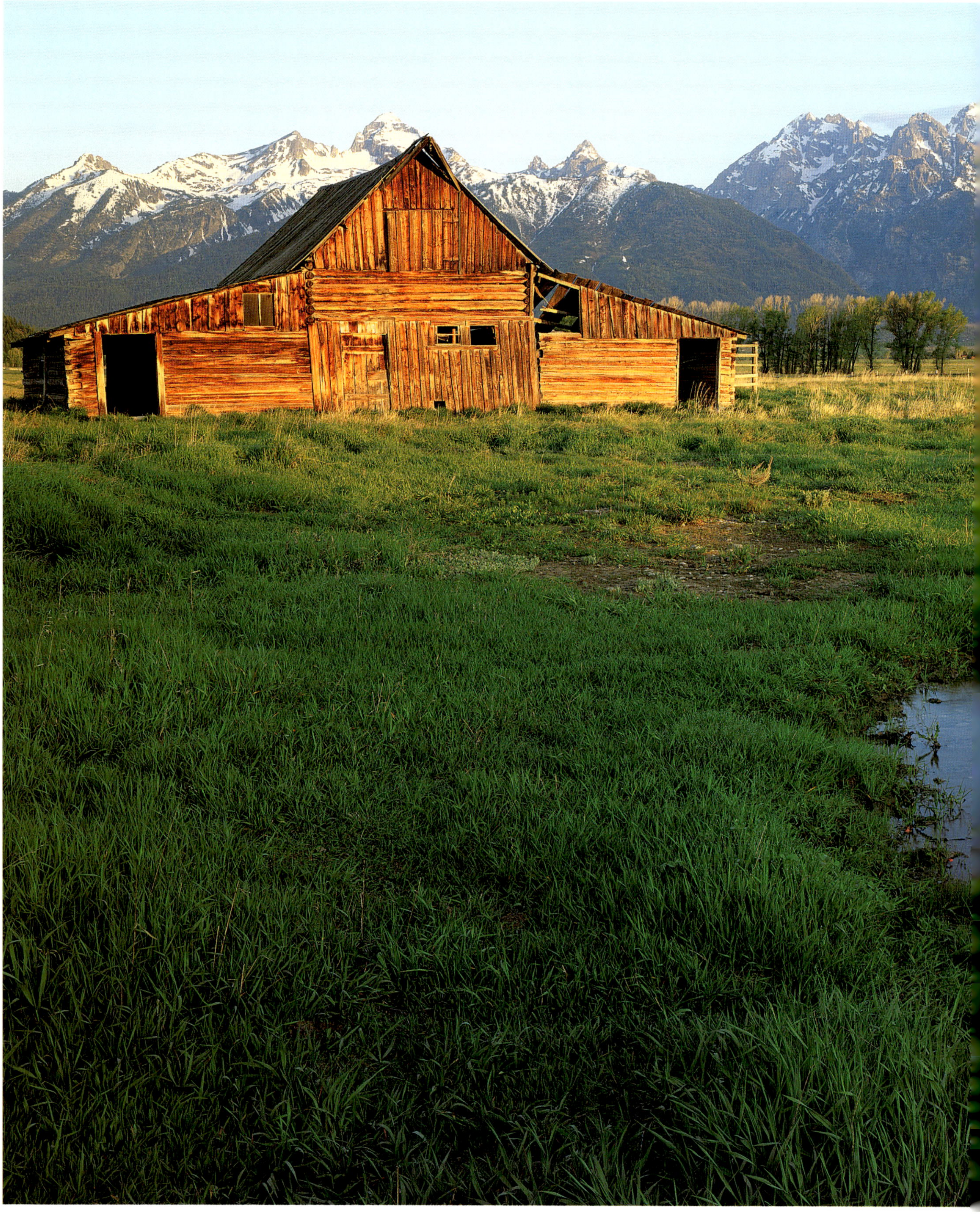

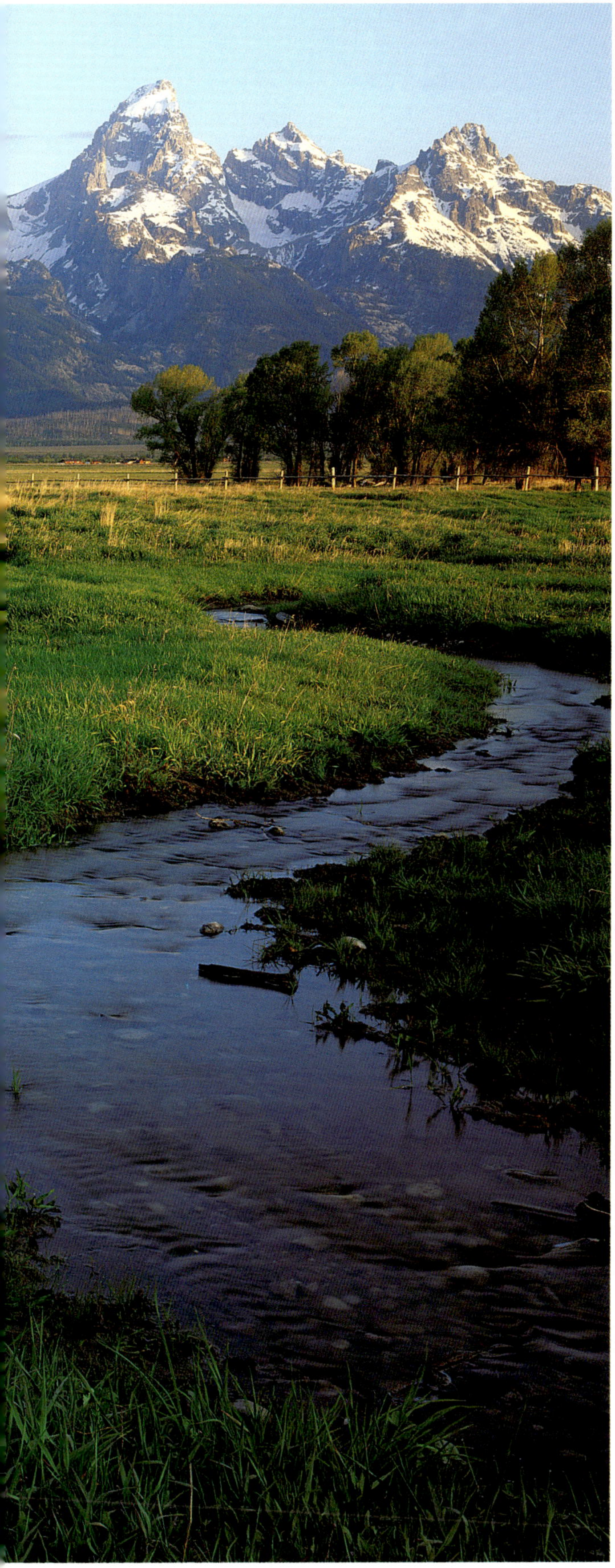

DIANA STRATTON

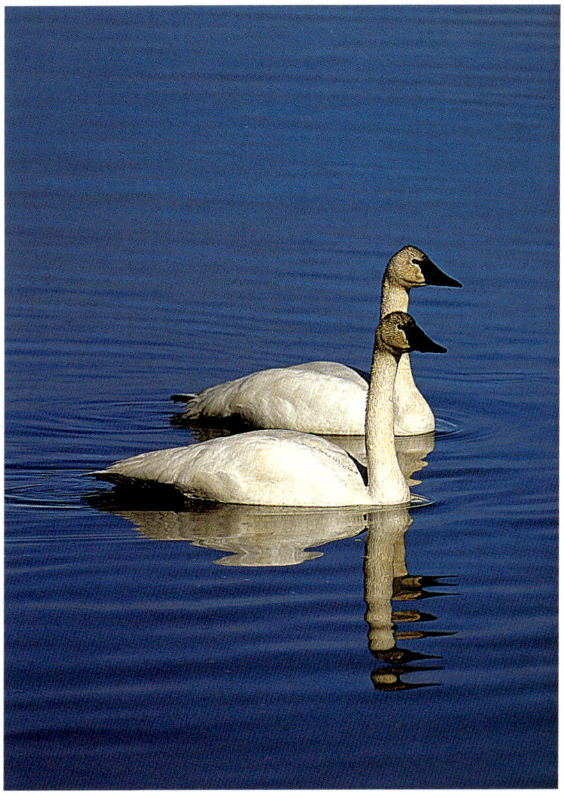

DIANA STRATTON

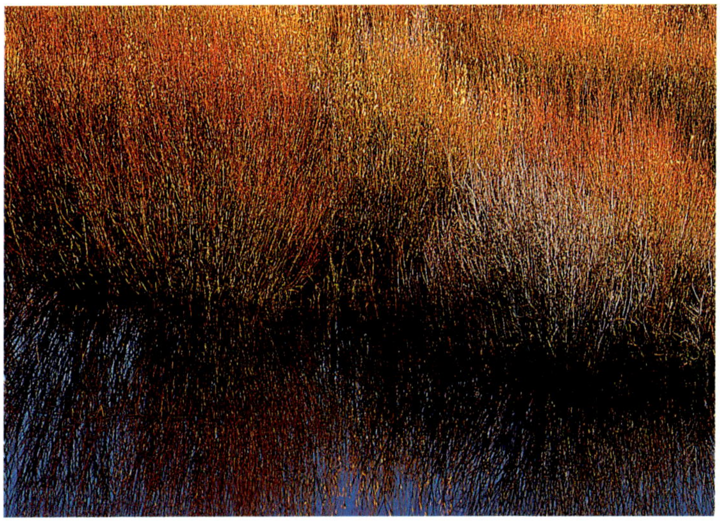

Above: Autumn transforms willows in Grand Teton National Park.

Top: Trumpeter swan pair on a pond in the National Elk Refuge.

Left: Historic barn, a favorite subject of photographers, is on the Moulton Ranch in Jackson Hole.

from the northern slope of Sheep Mountain, also called Sleeping Indian, on the edge of the Gros Ventres. People speculate that days of rain had saturated the mountain's sedimentary rock and soil, which let loose when triggered by an earth tremor. Whatever the cause, it took less than three minutes to scoop out a mile-long scar, which is still visible from much of Jackson Hole. To get a perspective on the magnitude of the Gros Ventre Slide, it is worth taking an hour side-trip to the site less than four miles east of Kelly and up the Gros Ventre Road.

But Mother Nature was not content with that act. Two years later, after a long period of rain, the dam, which was created by the earthen avalanche across the Gros Ventre River, burst. The resulting flood drowned six people and destroyed all of the up-and-coming town of Kelly, except for the school and Episcopal church. Farther downstream, the flood wiped out the approaches to the Snake River Bridge near Wilson and destroyed the Imeson Bridge at Hoback Junction.

Wildlife

With an elevation change of more than 6,000 feet from valley floor to highest surrounding peaks, Jackson Hole is a layer cake of diverse habitats. These habitats range from riparian along the streams and lakes, through sagebrush and grass, and on up through the conifer and aspen stands, to alpine niches where pikas and marmots forage their brief season among boulder fields.

There are hundreds of flowers, grasses, shrubs, and trees in Jackson Hole. We each have our favorite plants by which we mark the season and the year. We remember when the balsamroot formed a blanket of yellow on hillsides down Hog Island way, when the heart-leaf arnica failed to blossom in Phillips Canyon; when the shooting stars could not be counted, when the monkshood towered over our heads. For many of us, recognizing the native plants and their seasons means we are fully part of this place and have resided here long enough to gather such knowledge. We watch for signs of the season: the aspen greening the Wilson Faces in the spring or gold-plating Skyline Hill in the fall, the buttercup pushing through the snow near Moose at the end of winter, the huckleberry ripening in Black Canyon in the summer.

Although 305 species of birds and 49 species of mammals have been recorded on the National Elk Refuge alone, few reptiles and amphibians can survive Jackson Hole winters. Still, to our delight, frogs serenade us for a week or two each summer from the Hardeman meadows, and garter snakes dart across the trail to Phelps Lake. The fish may not be as numerous as they were even sixty years ago–let alone when the first trappers happened on this valley–but cutthroat trout continue to entice and outsmart today's anglers at stream and lake.

Two sets of biologist brothers are associated with seminal studies of wildlife in the Jackson Hole and Yellowstone ecosystems: half brothers Olaus and Adolph Murie and identical twins Frank and John Craighead. Both pairs of brothers arrived to study the wildlife of the region, but as soon as they could, they bought land in the Moose area and began raising families. In the intervening years, the Muries and the Craigheads have profoundly influenced both local and national understanding of this place, in particular, and of ecology, in general. Olaus Murie's *The Elk of North America* is *the* textbook work on the second largest member of the deer family. *Wapiti Wilderness*, co-authored by Murie and his wife, Mardy, remains to this day a wonderful portrayal of the valley as it was in the 1920s and 1930s, as well as a testament to the spirit of conservation.

In the summer of 1934, John and Frank Craighead had all the time in the world to get from their home in Washington, D.C. to Wyoming. After descending Togwotee Pass into Jackson Hole, Frank Craighead said, "We got a sight of the Tetons and we knew we were really in the mountains."

But what impressed him as much as the ramparts of the Tetons were the fish: a teeming mass of cutthroat trout rising to a hatch of insects. Having grown up next to the Potomac River and watching its slow deterioration, Craighead hoped, even in the 1930s, that he could do something to keep the same from befalling the Snake and other rivers in the West. "Here was a chance to do it right," he said. To that end, he and his brother devoted themselves, in the early years, to studying raptors–golden eagles, goshawks and prairie falcons–and wildflowers; in their later years, they turned to Canada geese, grizzly bears and elk.

In addition to publishing scientific papers and stories in *National Geographic* over the past four decades, the Craighead brothers have written popular books. Some of their findings have been controversial, including a recommendation that grizzlies in Yellowstone National Park be fed to keep them away from campgrounds when the use of accessible garbage dumps ended. Frank Craighead's best-known book is *The Track of the Grizzly*. *A Field Guide To Rocky Mountain Wildflowers* was co-authored by the brothers and Ray J. Davis. The book, one of the Peterson Field Guide Series, contains color photographs augmented with drawings by Jackson Hole artist Grant "Tiny" Hagen.

By 1959, the Craigheads were able to live year-round in cabins they had built on land purchased from original Mormon Row homesteader John Moulton. From the Craighead compound of houses and cabins directly east of the Grand, it is not uncommon to observe forty to fifty elk traveling through nearby fields, nor to have moose, deer, antelope, pocket gophers, pack rats and snowshoe hare approach the door, or trumpeter swans and bald eagles fly over the roof. "The bison we're not too thrilled about," admits Shirley Craighead, Frank's wife, "because they knock over our trees."

"The main difference here is that you can see a lot of these animals, as compared to parts of Alaska [which has more animals, but] where the vegetation is so dense," Frank Craighead said. "Any time you see a large number of animals together over a period of time, it makes an impression."

Many of the animals–bird and mammal–we see in Jackson Hole are migrants, intent on finding nesting and feeding grounds. Thousands of song birds and waterfowl travel through the valley each year, coming and going, in waves and in pairs, as insects and plants appear and disappear, as water in streams and lakes thaws and freezes. Their names evoke color and sound and flight patterns: cliff swallow, lazuli bunting, meadowlark, and yellow warbler; cinnamon teal, cormorant, osprey, and merganser. These birds can be seen from any highway or lane: mountain bluebirds on the Gros

CHERYL R. RICHTER

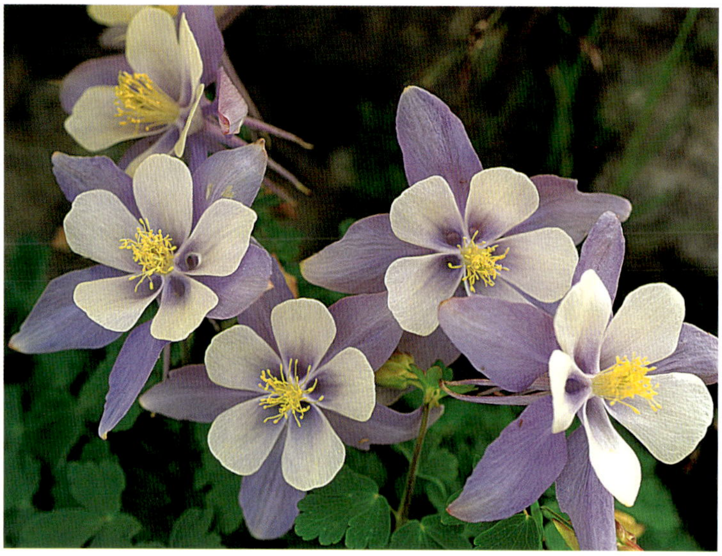

Above: Colorado blue columbine, once abundant throughout the Rocky Mountains, has become harder to find.

Right: Sunrise on Mount Moran.

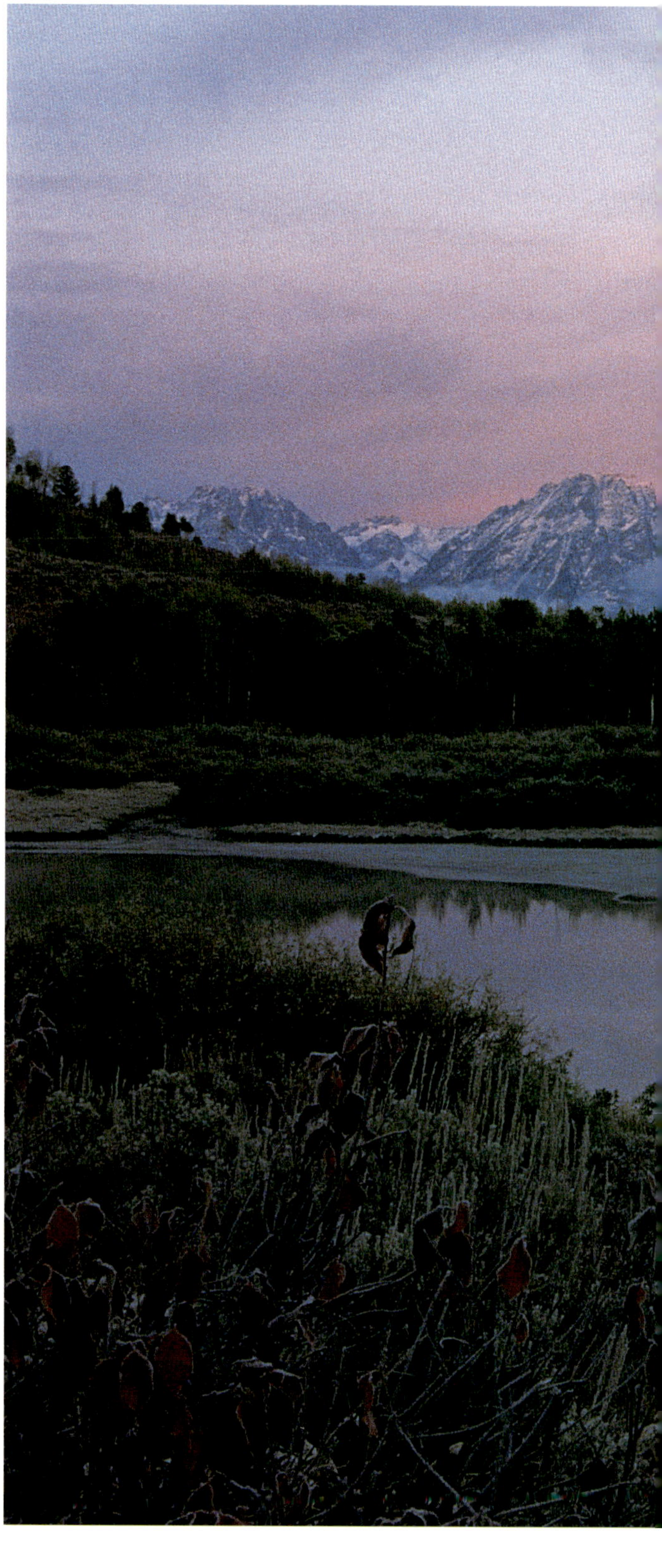

PERRY W. CONWAY

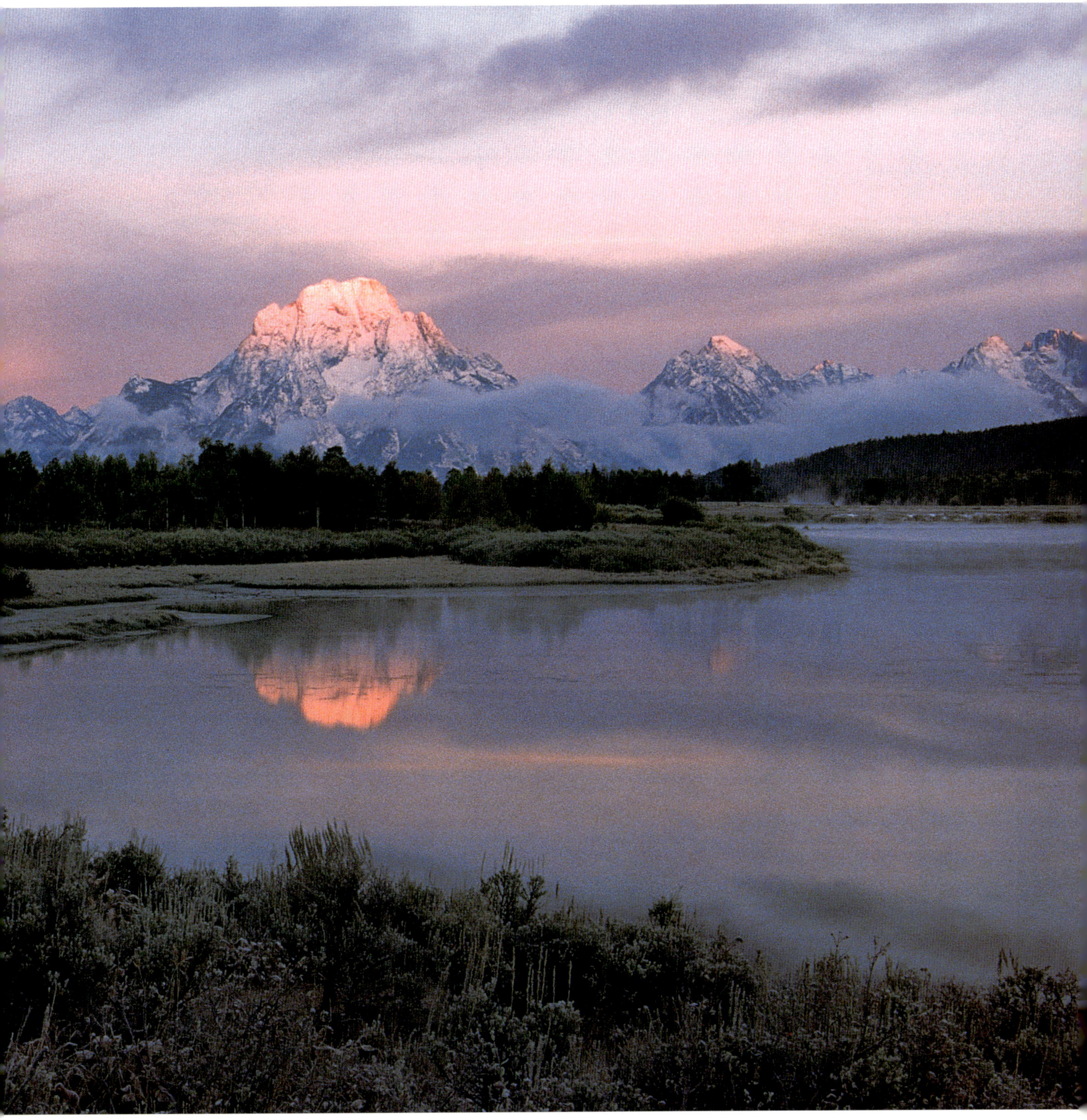

Ventre Road to Kelly in early spring, great blue herons in the Hardeman fields near Wilson. Frank Craighead's most recent book, *For Everything There Is A Season*, offers insights about the conjunction of animals, insects, and plants to be expected seasonally in Jackson Hole and Yellowstone.

"There's a lot we don't know about the migrations," said Craighead. "Most of the birds right around here come back within a day or two of the year before." When we spot Canada geese or swans, we cannot always assume spring has come or that winter is around the corner. Some birds, like snow geese, come from as far away as Alaska, stopping here only briefly on their more epic journey. Others, like redtail hawks, may leave for a couple of months, going only as far as the Wasatch Mountains in Utah to winter. Some birds, like ravens, magpies and black capped chickadees, are permanent residents around our homes. Others, like soaring flocks of white pelicans above the Snake River, tempt us to follow their lead and attain a loftier perspective of the country.

Migrations are ecologically important because they distribute animals throughout their ranges and throughout the seasons, according to Bruce Smith, local biologist with the United States Fish and Wildlife Service. Such movement allows vegetation and prey to mature through cycles of growth and decay, birth and death, and increases the animals' general fitness and the population's gene pool. If birds and mammals remained in the valley and mountains the entire year, plants and prey within the limited ranges could be destroyed, threatening the animals' physical well-being and survival as a species.

The National Elk Refuge

If you mention Jackson Hole to outsiders, images of mountains and skiing immediately come to mind. But, the discussion is likely to include the National Elk Refuge, too. It sprawls north of the town of Jackson, attracting people from as far away as Australia and China who come to see the elk, or wapiti, as they are also known. In the late fall and throughout the winter, sight of the elk on the refuge frequently compels motorists on adjacent Highway 26 to stop. And, during the winter, people can get even closer to the elk via sleigh; as many as 35,000 people in one winter have ridden the refuge on a sleigh.

"Elk are fascinating animals," said biologist Bruce Smith. "They are beautiful creatures with their dark manes and reddish coats. And, of course, there are the antlers." Added to the aesthetic qualities are other attractions: the elks' sociability–highly gregarious compared to more solitary deer and moose–and their bugling and fighting during the fall rut, that time when bulls convince cows of their suitability as mates.

Nobody knows for certain how many elk in the past have lived in the Jackson Hole and Yellowstone areas. Some say as many as 60,000 roamed the region during the 19th century, while others estimate a more conservative total of 25,000 in the various herds. At the beginning of the 20th century, the entire elk population in North America had been reduced to 50,000; but by the late 1990s, that number had increased to 900,000, thanks to efforts by conservation and hunting groups. Of the estimated 16,000 elk residing in Grand Teton and Yellowstone national parks, the Gros Ventre Mountains to the east, and the Teton Wilderness to the northeast, an average of 7,500 head winter on the refuge's 24,000 acres.

"They are not truly what they were at one time," Smith said, "but they give us glimpses of what the West must have been like 150 years ago."

The primary motive behind the establishment of the refuge in 1912 was the local community's desire to prevent elk from starving to death because fences and buildings barred them from migrating to traditional feeding areas. Further prompting the conservation effort was concern that the elk might be slaughtered to extinction. The Department of the Interior in 1910 assisted by purchasing 2,000 acres and allocating $20,000 for feeding elk that year. Over the next twenty-four years, private groups, such as the Izaak Walton League, raised funds to buy additional land, and by 1935 the refuge reached its current size.

For all its good intentions, the practice of winter feeding and protecting elk in Jackson Hole has a down side. The practice has continued with only a few interruptions since World War II. Before 1950, Smith explained, only 800 elk summered in Grand Teton National Park; now, there are between 4,000 and 5,000 elk in the park. With winter mortality down, as many as 1,000 new elk can be added each season. That increase comes despite uncertainty about the carrying capacity of the habitat, especially as the human population encroaches. The animal is unable to migrate elsewhere and carnivores that historically helped control elk herds are missing from the area. The U.S. Fish and Wildlife Service and the Wyoming Game and Fish Department have concluded that the optimum size of the Jackson Hole elk herd is 11,000 head.

One way of dealing with overpopulation has been to allow hunting on the refuge and in the park, when the animals migrate in late October and November from the higher meadows. "We never harvest as many as we want," Smith said. "The elk are getting smarter and the hunters aren't." He referred to the elk traveling in herds and at night when they cannot be hunted. The reduction hunt continues to foment controversy because it occurs so close to public roads and because some perceive that the elk are nothing but sitting ducks in a shooting gallery.

"Given a choice, we wouldn't feed elk," Smith added. However, he also knows the prospect of thousands of starving elk so close to town would not set well with either resident or visitor, hunter or animal lover.

Elk are not the only spectacular creatures to frequent the refuge. On a single day as many as 270 trumpeter swans–distinctive with their black bills–have been counted. Trumpeters from as far away as southern Montana have wintered on the open water of Flat Creek marsh and on Miller and Winegar springs. Despite miles of ice-free water along the Snake River, the swans prefer the refuge because of the rich plants that grow in the muck. Although two pairs of swans have nested along Flat Creek, the U.S. Fish and Wildlife Service since 1987 has built new ponds to entice more.

In addition to elk and swans, the refuge and Jackson Hole shelter other ungulates, such as mule deer, American bison, pronghorn antelope, moose, and bighorn sheep. Some of these, such as the bison and antelope, are common sights on the refuge road toward Curtis Canyon or on Antelope Flats Road skirting Blacktail Butte in the Park.

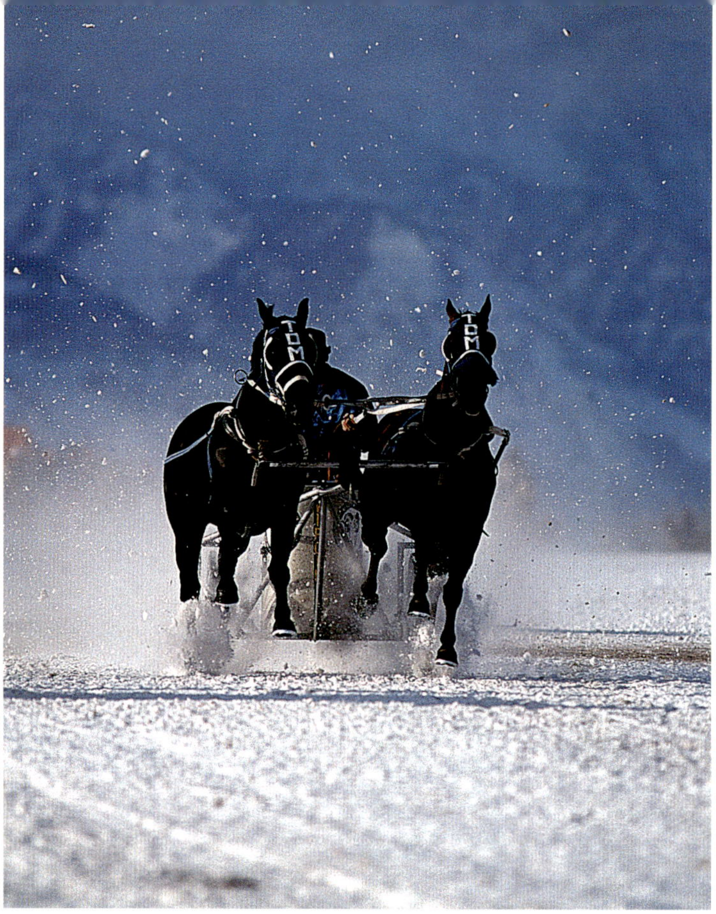

Right: Cutter races are among annual events in January and February in Jackson Hole.

Below: From Signal Mountain, the Teton Range is girdled in fog.

HENRY H. HOLDSWORTH

GLENN VAN NIMWEGEN

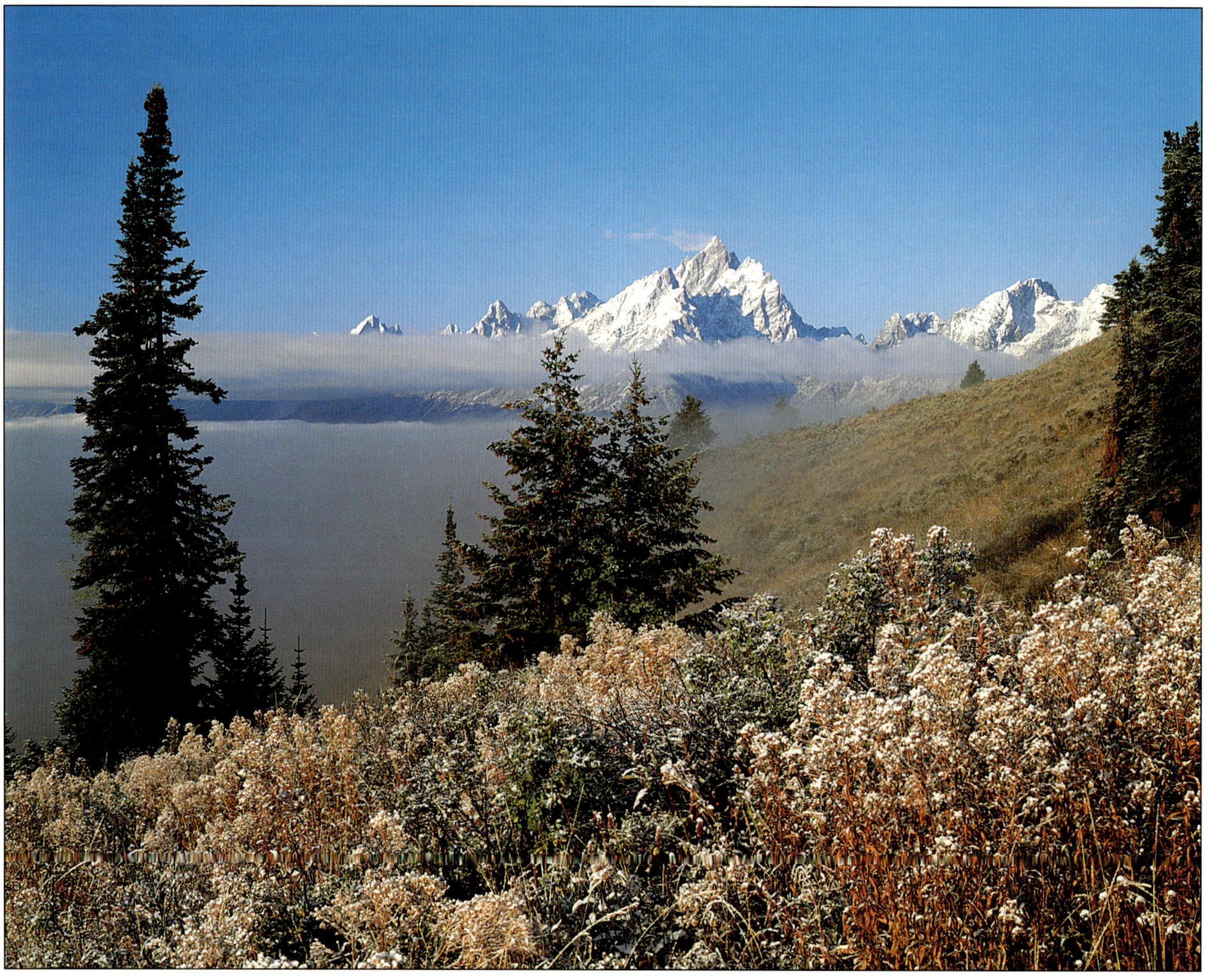

W. PERRY CONWAY

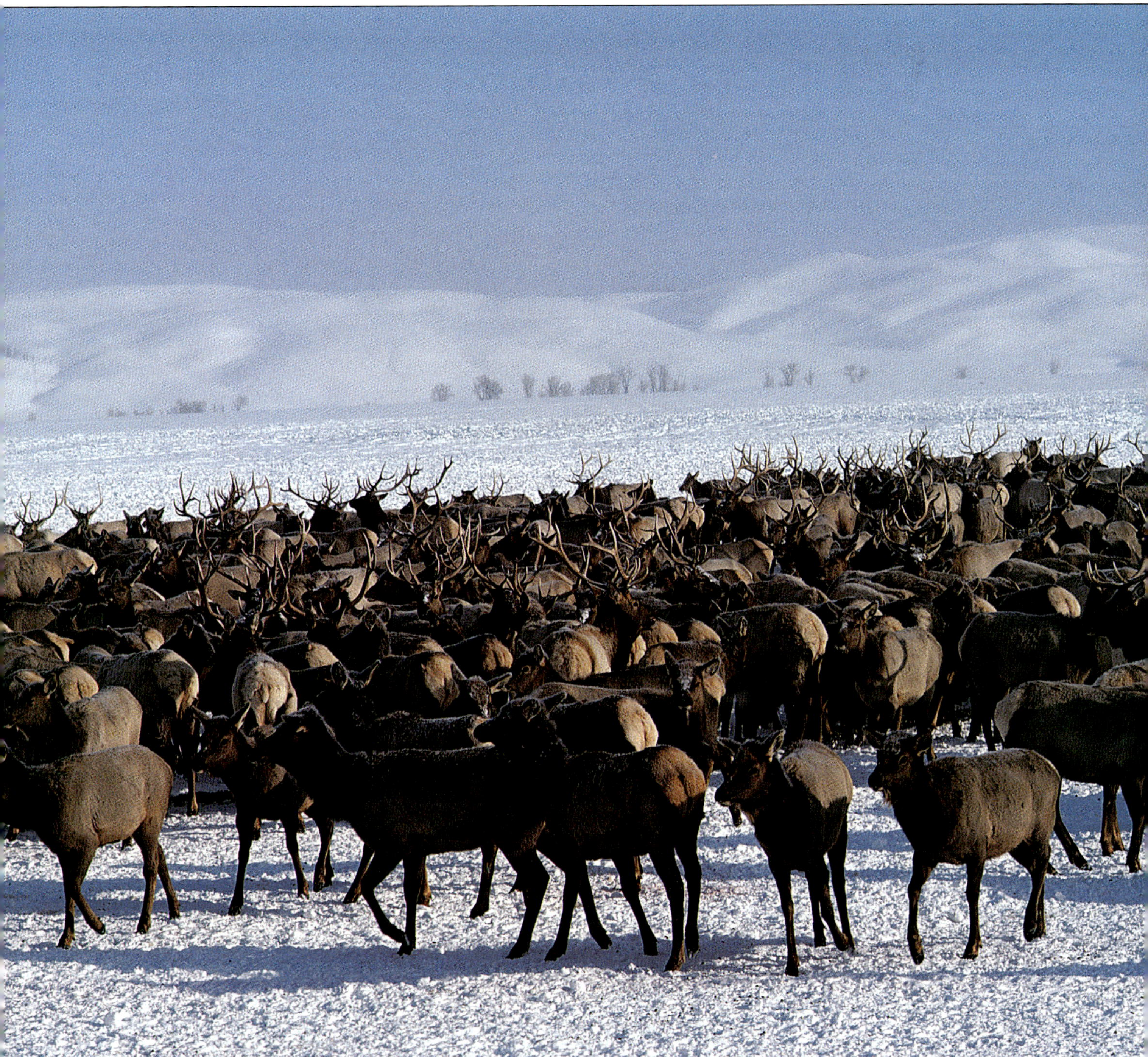

The National Elk Refuge provides feed and sanctuary for about 7,500 head each winter.

Beaver, otter, marten, snowshoe hare, ermine, and black bear are more difficult to observe, but can be seen at dawn and dusk far from the pavement. Local tour companies and educational institutions, such as Great Plains Wildlife Institute and Teton Science School, offer services increasing a visitor's chances of glimpsing wildlife.

Changing Times

Although hunting has become essential to maintain the health of wildlife, carnivores traditionally were the important ingredient in the well-being of these animals. For that reason, the federal government reintroduced the wolf into the Yellowstone ecosystem. Such a notion has not always prevailed and is still anathema in some circles. Grand Teton National Park superintendent's reports from the 1930s read like a "litany of how many varmints were killed," said public affairs officer Linda Olson. "Doe-eyed ungulates were favored over predators. Our ideas of ecology have changed."

Plenty of coyotes still rove Jackson Hole, but Smith was excited to spot a female mountain lion and two kittens on the refuge during a recent winter. Friends running and hiking in Cache Creek east of Jackson and up the Gros Ventre River have seen mountain lions as well. In 1994, a grizzly sow and two cubs wandered, apparently following the Snake River, to a point a couple miles south of the Wilson Bridge.

Some of us are not always enthusiastic at the prospect of meeting a large solitary predator or packs of carnivores. Whether it be reintroduced wolves from Yellowstone or a grizzly near Two Ocean Lake, when they show up in our backyards or along a trail we want to hike, we may find it inconvenient or life-threatening. When the human population meets carnivores, such as coyotes and the protected grizzly, contact means conflict, and death–more often for the animal than for the person. One of the grizzly cubs spotted on the Snake River drowned after being tranquilized. In the mid-1980s, a grizzly sow, who had been getting into trash at Togwotee Lodge, was mistakenly shot a few weeks later by a hunter up Granite Creek.

For ranchers especially, the predators are not a welcome sight. When ranchers and carnivores try to occupy the same area, predation by the wild animals threatens livelihoods and lives. Between 1990 and 1995 the United States Fish and Wildlife Service reported sixty grizzlies were killed by people within the Yellowstone ecosystem, an area which incorporates Jackson Hole and its critical bear habitat.

Even the elk and bison are perceived as a threat to the ranchers because they carry brucellosis, a bacterium that causes spontaneous abortions in livestock and wildlife. Most of the political and economic blame for the disease being potentially transmitted to livestock has landed on the bison, and hundreds of the animals have been shot upon leaving Yellowstone National Park. However, elk have been indicted as possible culprits as well. Additional studies are needed on brucellosis and how it may be transmitted to cattle; ironically, the disease was initially passed from the domestic animals to the wild ungulates. Smith has recommended keeping cattle off elk range until well after the latter have calved, thus lessening the chance that the disease will be spread between the animals.

Shared Space

At a visceral level, we are all pleased to see a bull elk, his great rack silhouetted against the Sleeping Indian mountain, or an otter slicing the darkening water at the Oxbow Bend on the Snake River near Moran But even when these less-threatening animals interrupt our travel or prevent us from building where we want or interfere with our work, we may be less than pleased with their presence, and act accordingly.

Despite the often negative outcome of human and animal interactions within the same habitat, we still relish wildlife and flowers at close quarters in Jackson Hole. Smith tells the story of one Christmas Eve in Jackson: "We had a big picture window with a table and a poinsettia on it. We looked out and here was this moose, nose pressed against the window, working its lips and tongue, trying to get that plant. She and her calf bedded down that night under the golden willows [in the yard]."

Opportunities to see wildlife could become less commonplace. In 1994, 3,700,000 people visited Grand Teton National Park, up considerably from the 2,100,000 in 1963. "April is the only month to breathe," said Linda Olson, park spokeswoman. The park grapples daily with how much the landscape can stand before the people and the animals, the plants and the very rocks say, "Uncle. Enough. No more."

All those people migrating to Jackson Hole means the wildlife habitat has been whittled down by fences and houses, by recreational and domestic activities. "If they lose enough habitat," Frank Craighead said, "the species is threatened. It's quite possible under adverse environmental conditions, there would be large losses or it would take a long time for the animals to recover." Despite his desire and effort to see our ecosystem remain untrammeled, he said, "You could see the changes were coming pretty rapidly. In the early 1950s, we proposed a river management program to set aside wild and scenic rivers."

Although the number of birds in Jackson Hole has declined since the 1930s, Craighead pointed out that some species are more adaptable to human beings and have actually increased with settlement and the growing number of visitors. He points out that ravens have multiplied at the expense of hawks. The ravens don't mind our structures and our trash, nor do they feel the loss of small mammals and rodents on which raptors prey, or the destruction of nesting areas. Canada geese also have increased dramatically because they are compatible with people's lawns and pools of water.

Roads and wildlife especially do not mix. Deer, elk and moose are accustomed to traveling at dusk, when visibility is the poorest; during winter the problem is exacerbated by fog and blowing snow. The private feeding of deer, elk and moose also aggravates the problem. Sensing that the animals are starving, people have put hay out near roads. After a few years, the animals know where to find browse and will cross busy highways to get it.

According to Wyoming Game and Fish Department reports, more than 235 deer, twelve moose, and forty-five elk were killed by cars and trucks in Jackson Hole between 1989-1995; this number does not reflect those that are hit and wander away from the road to die. Hardly a day goes by during the winter without seeing a deer

DIANA STRATTON

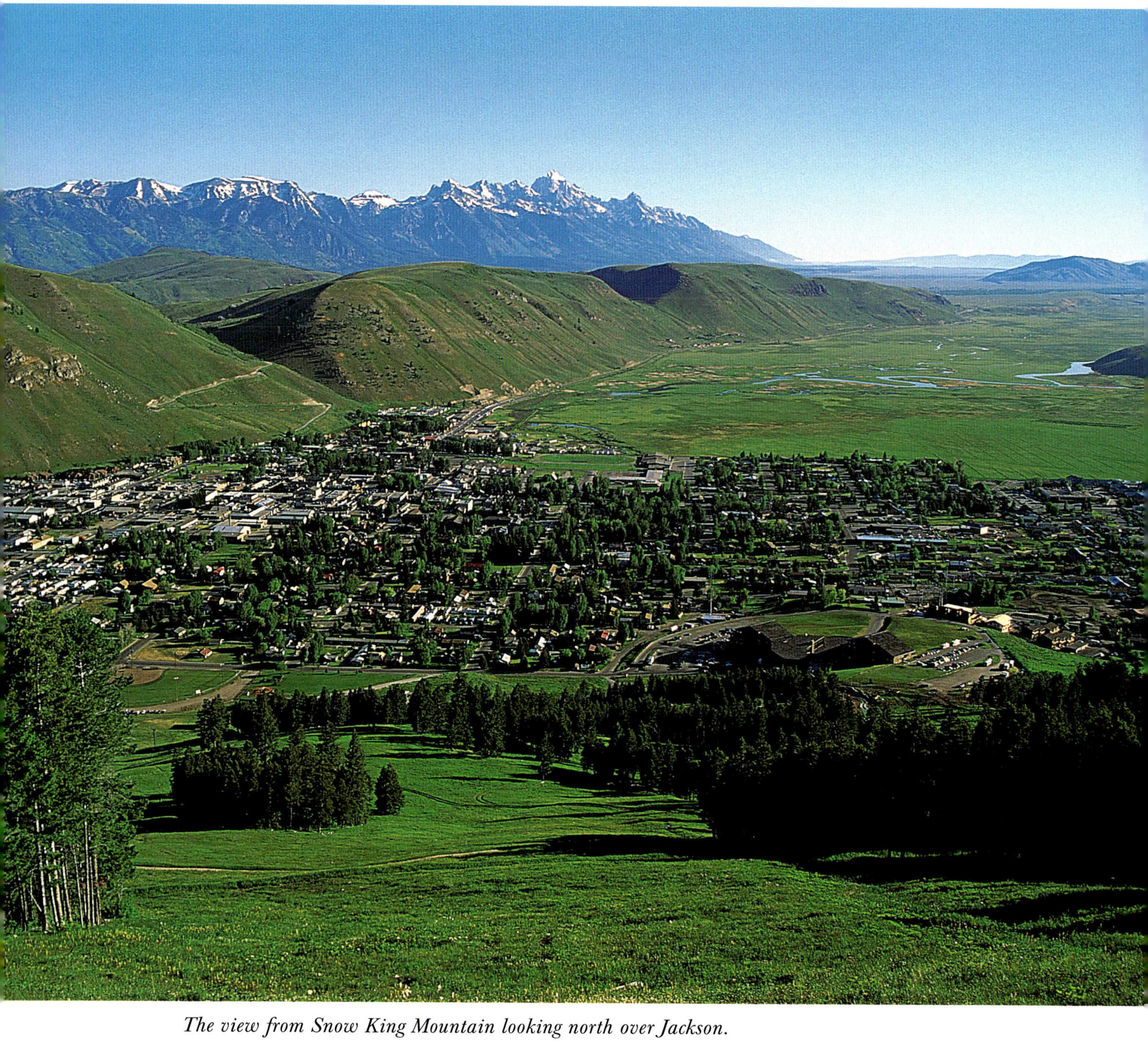

The view from Snow King Mountain looking north over Jackson.

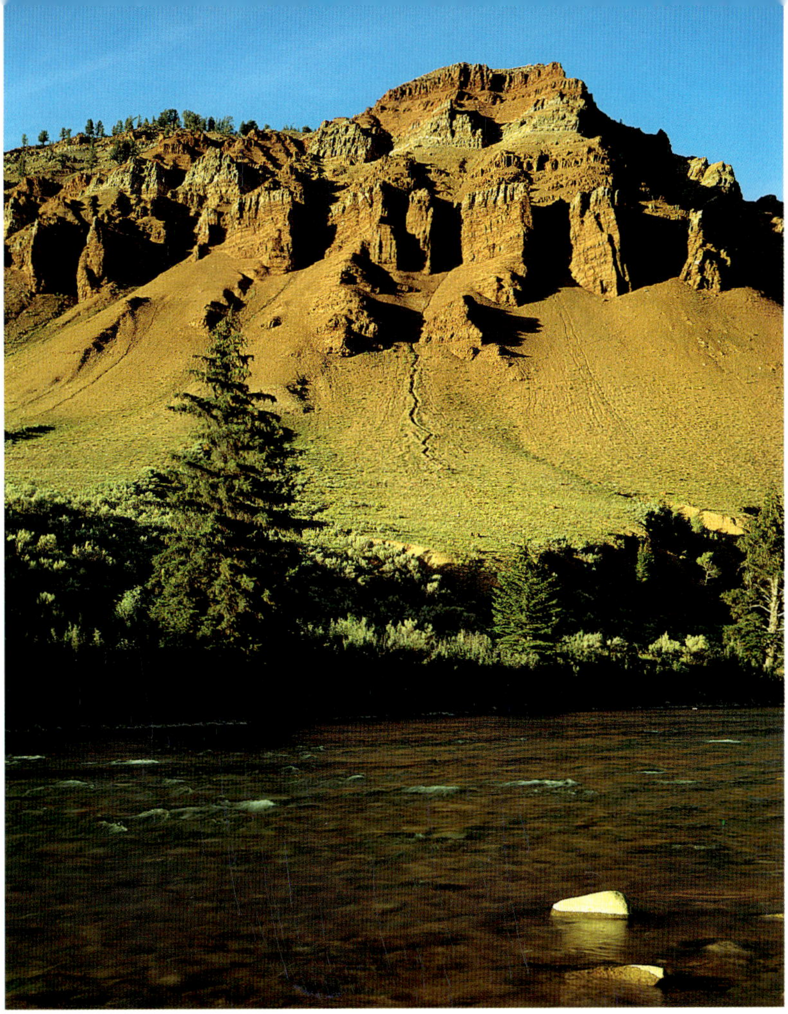

GLENN VAN NIMWEGEN

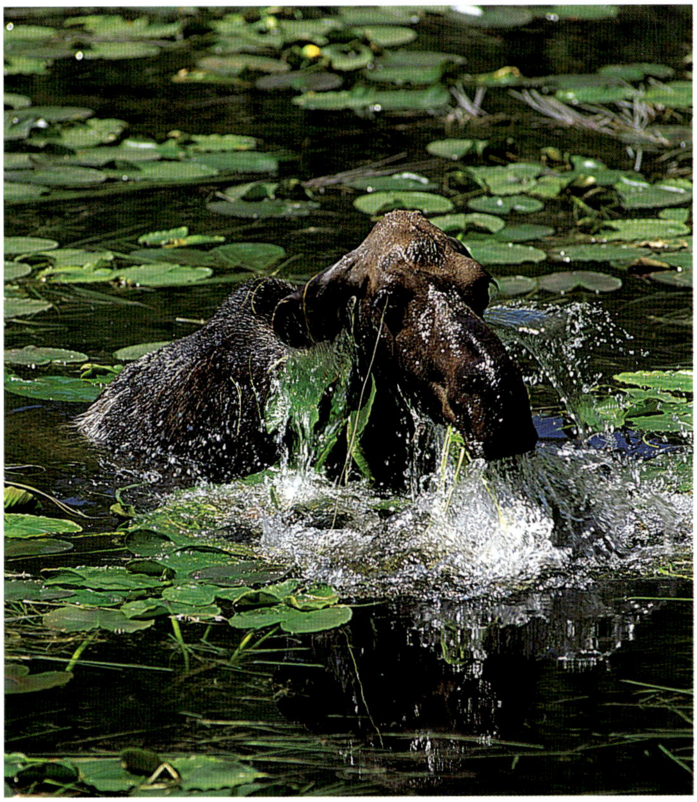

GLENN VAN NIMWEGEN

Above: The Gros Ventre River flows through the Red Hills area near Jackson.

Left: Cow moose makes a meal of lily stalks in a pond in Grand Teton National Park.

carcass being scavenged by ravens on the road between Jackson and the outlying communities. Public and private agencies and individuals started a campaign in 1995 to heighten awareness of the problem.

Ultimately, how we interact with the animals and the plant life with which we share the land and water will convey to another generation and to visitors our sense of place, our feelings toward home. There is much we can be commended for. The formation of the National Elk Refuge started with the community responding to a perceived need. Cooperation between the refuge and the local Boy Scout troops has provided money both for feed for the elk and operating expenses for the youth group. Each spring the Boy Scouts walk the refuge and collect the antlers that the elk have shed. They then sell the antlers to artisans and aphrodisiac wholesalers from around the world at an auction every May on the Jackson Town Square.

Today, the community continues to respond to problems specific to this place. Since 1979, the Jackson Hole Alliance for Responsible Planning has been trying to figure out ways people and wildlife can coexist. Frank Craighead's son, Charlie, is pulling together the stories of how people and animals do and don't live well together. Beginning in 1980, the Jackson Hole Land Trust has helped to preserve 7,926 acres ranch lands and wetlands in Teton County; additional acreage has been set aside in scenic easements as well by The Nature Conservancy and Teton County.

Forging workable solutions for integrating people, wildlife and plants, within a habitat that supports all of us, is perhaps the largest issue facing our community; we can be players or partners. The problem is being addressed throughout the Rocky Mountains, where similar rural communities are at a crossroads. Linda Olson has many reasons for living in this place, but foremost among them is "seeing a big old moose tromping around." Not one of us wants that big old moose to disappear because of literal and figurative fences between people. Not one of us wants that big old moose to become nothing more than a memory. For Bruce Smith, the elk "represent things that are less and less common. They have a place here. They do something for us spiritually as well as materially."

Getting Here

Getting to Jackson Hole–the valley that incorporates more than Grand Teton National Park and the town of Jackson–has not always been as simple as it is today. In the 1990s, anybody can book a flight through Delta or United from New York City or Kathmandu, or pull out a United States road atlas, and trace a route along interstates and country roads from Los Angeles or Pittsburgh. Interstate 90 is only four hours to the north and I-80 the same to the south, while U.S. 26 connects the valley to Idaho Falls, Idaho, 100 miles to the west and to Casper, Wyoming, 300 miles to the east.

Each summer, Winnebagos climb Teton Pass's ten percent grades and bike tourists pedal the winding curves of Hoback Canyon into the Hole. Other seasons, two-seater Cessnas, Boeing 737s, and Air Force One's fleet of helicopters and smaller jets navigate the approaches to land beneath vertiginous mountains, bringing President and ordinary folk to ski our peaks and fish our streams, to play a round of golf or sample our restaurants.

That has not always been the case. Landscape and weather, economics and history have conspired to keep people out of–or to hold them captive in–the Hole. A "hole" was the 19th century fur trapper's designation for any mountain-locked valley. Once, there were summers when automobiles had to be pulled by horses over Teton Pass, and there were winters when the snow fell with such vehemence that everyone decided to hibernate.

With the valley floor more than 6,000 feet above sea level, the Jackson Hole basin can make an inhospitable terrain for the ill-prepared. People–from the community of Moran at the northern end of the Hole to the village of Hoback Junction at the southern–pride themselves on surviving temperatures of forty degrees below zero, snowdrifts that bury fence and truck, and years when the pantry held only elk meat and crackers. Surrounded by buttes, ridges and peaks ranging from 1,000 to nearly 8,000 feet over our heads, Jackson Holers find themselves up against an almost impenetrable wall of startling rock in the west and a confusing assortment of hills and drainages to the north, east and south. Rivers, streams and lakes play their part as well in isolating people–rapids and steep canyons cutting them off from each other, from where they think they might rather be. Of course, such a challenging landscape offers its rewards: in every direction, mountains to climb and ski, rivers to run, lakes to fish.

Since recorded history people have set out to find Jackson Hole, only to get confused by the search. Such was the case of mountain man Jim Bridger, famous for his tracking skills, who failed to find the right pass into the valley and who later maintained incorrectly that the Snake River was impossible to ford.

For at least 10,000 years people have been passing through Jackson Hole, leaving fragments of their lives–rejected arrowheads and spear points of native obsidian–for another generation to interpret. Stone Age people ventured here to hunt deer and bighorn sheep, and to gather plants, including camas root on the northern shore of Jackson Lake. At the turn of the 21st century, people come here to hunt and gather as well.

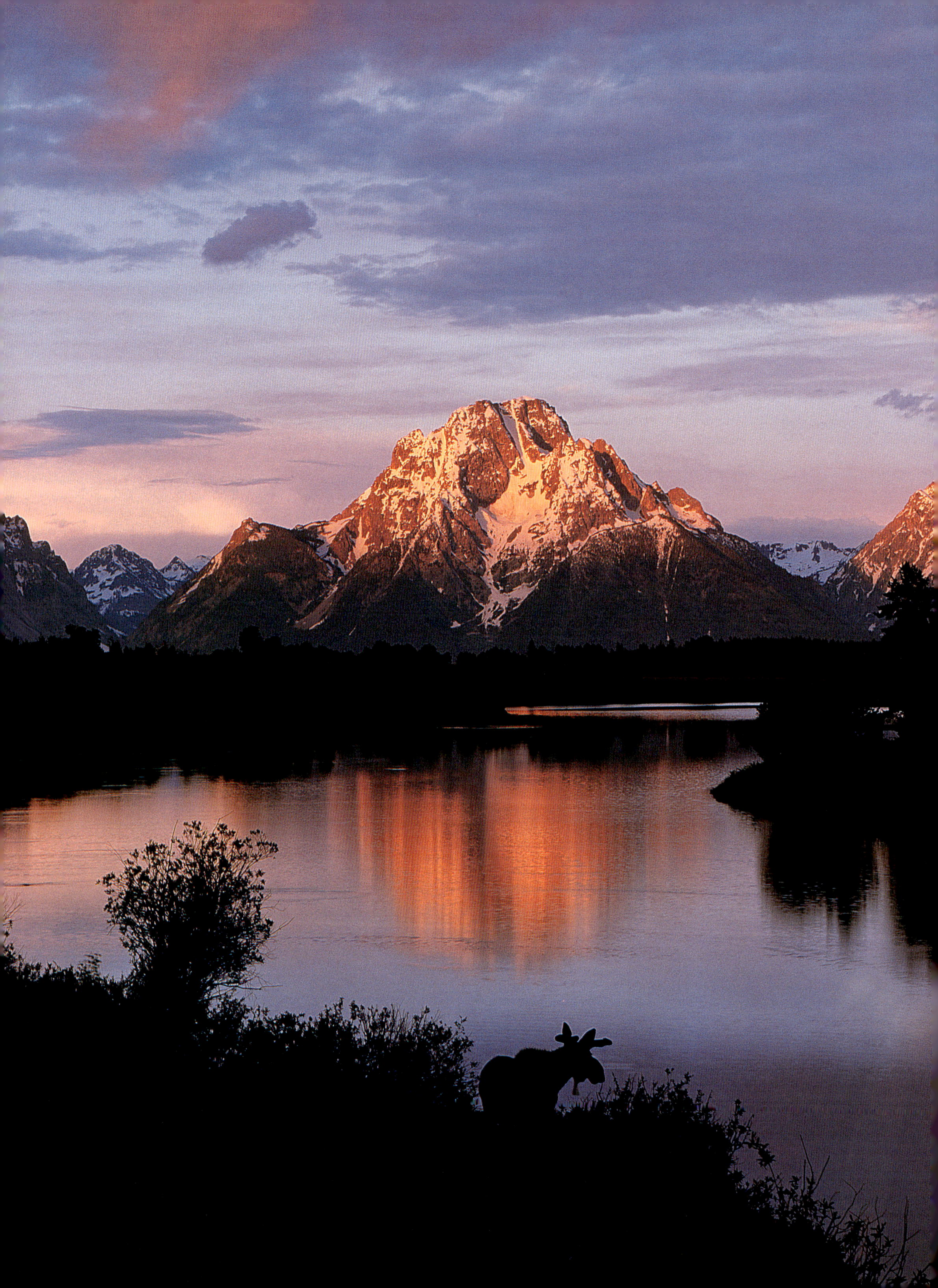

CHAPTER TWO

FROM TRAPPING TO SETTLEMENT

A modern crossroads exists in Jackson Hole, a crossroads that brings together people from different regions and economic backgrounds, with diverse cultural and spiritual leanings. People aspire to be first through the intersection, to make the most of the place–whether resident or visitor.

Although Native Americans left no written tales of Jackson Hole, amateur and professional archaeologists have found stone projectiles and knives that indicate prehistoric peoples ventured through Jackson Hole for almost 10,000 years. Beginning at the close of the Pinedale glaciation, early hunters and gatherers traveled throughout the Rocky Mountains, visiting Jackson Hole as recently as the 17th century. Sometime during this period, anthropologists speculate, these first Indian people were driven out of the territory by Shoshones, or Snake Indians. By the first years of the 1800s, none of the Indians in the area–the Blackfeet, Gros Ventres, Shoshones and Crows–were migrating through Jackson Hole. Because these tribes hunted on horseback and needed sufficient numbers of buffalo and other wild game, the journey into our valley was not worthwhile: the animals too few, the terrain too rugged.

Transient Trappers

Historian Merrill Mattes called Jackson Hole "the historic crossroads of the western fur trade." The trappers who made this valley a crossroads were affected as much by the desire to explore and exploit an unfamiliar world as by factors beyond their control–economics, politics, and wars. These factors egendered confict between white men and indigenous people, between trading companies, and between the desire to make profits and the need to preserve natural resources.

When the fur trappers started coming to this valley in the 1800s, they contended with the Gros Ventres and Blackfeet, who fought to keep the white intruders out. Explorer and trapper John Colter is famous in the annals of the West for reportedly running at least five miles to escape a group of Blackfeet intent on killing him.

During the 1830s, matters did not improve between brigades of trappers and Indians. The Battle of Pierre's Hole occurred just over Teton Pass during the summer of 1832, when as many as two dozen Gros Ventres were killed by a large contingent of trappers and their Flathead and Nez Perce allies. A week later, the Gros Ventres got revenge, killing three trappers who had crossed into Jackson Hole from the rendez-

Facing page: Moose in a sunset silhouette; Mount Moran catches the day's last rays. DIANA STRATTON

vous and were heading for the Hoback River canyon. Trapper Osborne Russell wrote in his *Journal* of an 1839 escape over Conant Pass from an Indian ambush near Jackson Lake.

Some trappers had less antagonistic relationships with indigenous peoples and married women from the various tribes. For Jackson Holers, the story of Richard "Beaver Dick" Leigh, his Shoshone wife, Jenny, and their children is familiar through the Englishman's diaries and letters. By 1863, Leigh was living in the valley as a trapper, hunter and guide; he helped guide the 1872 Hayden Expedition through the Tetons. Four years later he lost his family to smallpox.

By the close of the 19th century, treaties and smallpox had lessened the neighboring tribes' ability to wage war against the non-Indian invaders. The last reported battle between Indians and non-Indians in Jackson Hole was in July of 1895. *The New York Times* erroneously reported it as a "massacre." One Bannock Indian was killed, apparently because the homesteaders wanted to clear the valley of the Indians who hunted wild game "out of season" when the non-Indians could not.

Bannocks and Shoshones continued their summer migrations, at least into the 1920s and 1930s, traveling on horse or by wagon between the Fort Hall Indian Reservation in Idaho and the Wind River Indian Reservation on the east side of the Continental Divide. Eva Sanford Topping told an interviewer that her Moose Head homestead was on the Indians' old campground. Today, the Bannocks have returned as dancers and drummers from Fort Hall and participate in the Old West Days celebration.

John Colter, John Astor and the Fur Companies

A native Virginian, John Colter, is honored by legend as the first white man to visit Jackson Hole. He had been a member of the Lewis and Clark expedition, but by 1807 he was working as a guide for Manuel Lisa, a fur trader based in St. Louis. Lisa and all other fur traders were intent on capitalizing on the passion for beaver hats and hoped to find the animal in abundance in the West. In late November 1807, he ordered Colter to reconnoiter the area west and south of the confluence of the Yellowstone and Big Horn rivers, now south-central Montana, and to establish trading relations with Indian tribes in the region.

Because Colter neither made a map nor kept a journal of his explorations, his specific route continues to be debated by historians. Most believe he followed the Shoshone River to a thermal area near present-day Cody, "Colter's Hell." However, his passage over the Continental Divide and his first vantage of the Tetons can only be surmised. Some historians have ascribed to Colter a leisurely journey through Jackson Hole–awestruck as he must have been by the Tetons in the middle of winter–before leaving by way of Teton Pass at the southwestern boundary of the valley.

Whatever the truth, Colter undoubtedly saw the Tetons and explored enough of Jackson Hole to report the presence of beaver to Lisa. His journey presaged the beginning of extensive fur trapping operations throughout the Rocky Mountain West.

Between 1810 and the first trapper-trader rendezvous in 1825 on the Green River, individuals and small parties of trappers sporadically visited the area. In 1811, Jacob

Reznor, John Hoback and Edward Robinson, who had wintered in the Jackson Hole vicinity, guided the Astorians, trappers of John Jacob Astor's American Fur Company, through the area. The following year another party of Astorians reversed the journey, traveling west to east, and crossed the Continental Divide at South Pass at the southern end of the Wind River Mountains. Rather than following entirely what would become the Oregon Trail, they detoured through Jackson Hole–via Teton Pass and the Hoback River–to avoid skirmishes with Blackfeet and Crow. Continued Blackfeet resistance to the white men during this era forced fur trappers and traders to opt for more southerly routes, routes which inevitably took them through Jackson Hole.

Over the next seven years, although there was no concerted effort by trading companies to trap in Jackson Hole, the North West Company and Hudson's Bay Company probably sent employees into the area. By 1824, the Americans returned, this time with trapper and explorer Jedediah Smith at the head of a contingent of the Rocky Mountain Fur Company. His party followed the Hoback River into the valley and left via the Berry Creek drainage at the north end of Jackson Lake, crossing the Tetons at Conant Pass.

The Bible-toting Smith marked the beginning of a stream of legendary trappers and explorers that descended into Jackson Hole. The names of Jim Bridger, Hugh Glass, David E. Jackson, Kit Carson, William Sublette, and Osborne Russell make the roster of the brigades of the Rocky Mountain Fur Company, organized by Major Andrew Henry and William Ashley, and the American Fur Company. Before Ashley sold his interest in the Rocky Mountain Fur Company, he established the rendezvous, an annual event that allowed trappers to remain in the field, but brought them together with traders to exchange furs for supplies. It was the only time the outdoorsmen relaxed from the rigors of trapping, and they did it with zeal: drinking and dancing, swapping tales and news.

Rendezvous

The rendezvous still captures the imagination. Although none of these boisterous encampments gathered in Jackson Hole, the community stages its own re-creation of the event each Memorial Day weekend as part of Old West Days. Historically, rendezvous were held in Pierre's Hole on the western side of the Tetons, at the Popo Agie River on the east side of the Wind River Mountains, and most often along the Green River because of the easy access to South Pass and river routes east.

Between the 1826 rendezvous near the Great Salt Lake and the last rendezvous on Horse Creek in 1840, the trapping brigades crossed and recrossed Jackson Hole en route to the rendezvous, to attain new beaver grounds, to avoid Indian tribes, and to monitor their rivals' activities. In a business move reminiscent of an earlier one by the competing North West and Hudson's Bay companies, Astor's American Fur Company and the Rocky Mountain Fur Company divided up the region in 1833. They recognized that trapping beaver in the same area hurt both companies' profit margins. Astor's company ended up with the rights to Jackson Hole, and within three years, had monopolized the trade. But by 1838, it was apparent to the traders that the beaver

DIANA STRATTON

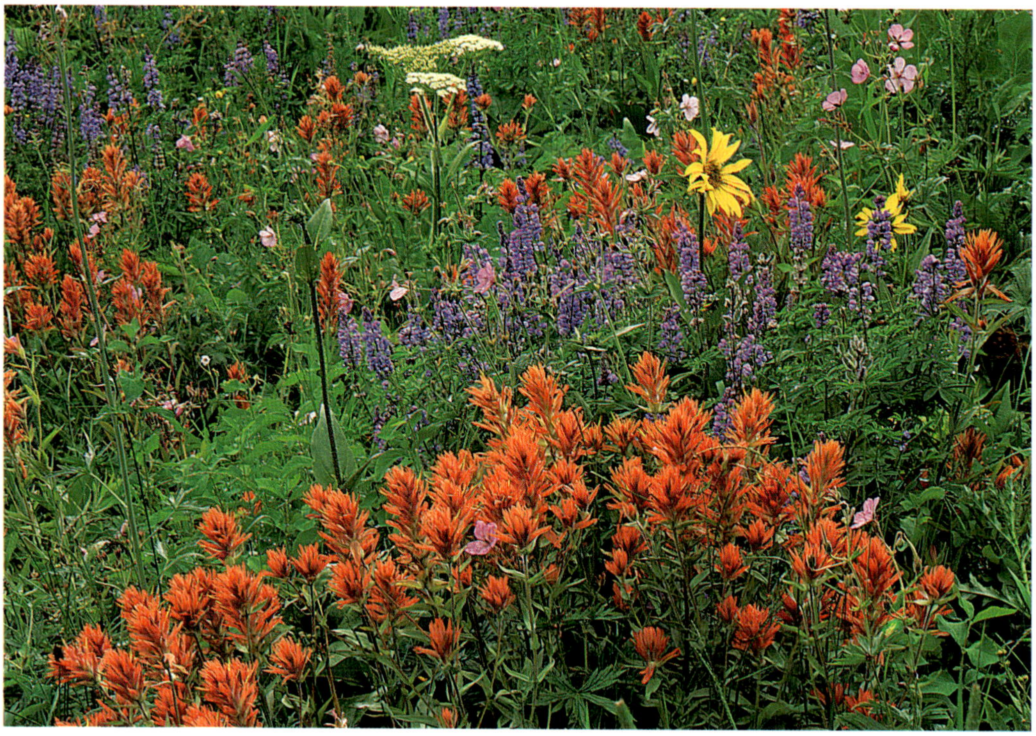

DIANA STRATTON

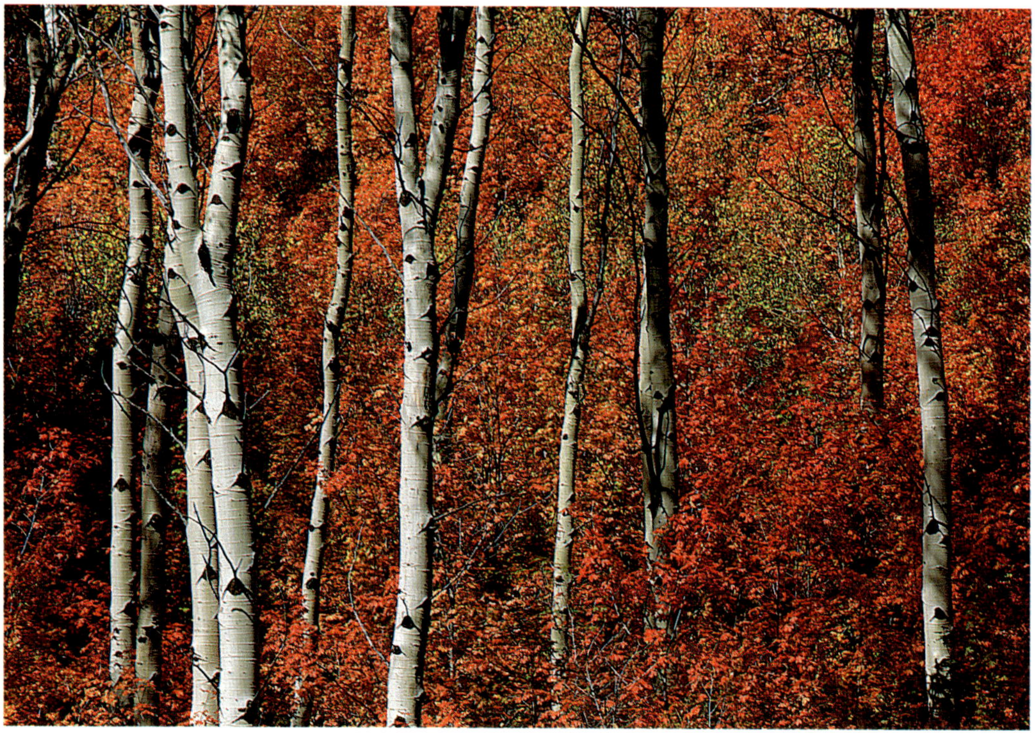

Above: Fall colors among the aspen in Jackson Hole appear electrified.

Top: Indian paintbrush and lupine decorate a slope in Grand Teton National Park.

Facing page: The Snake River winds toward a dramatic sunset behind the Teton Range.

W. PERRY CONWAY

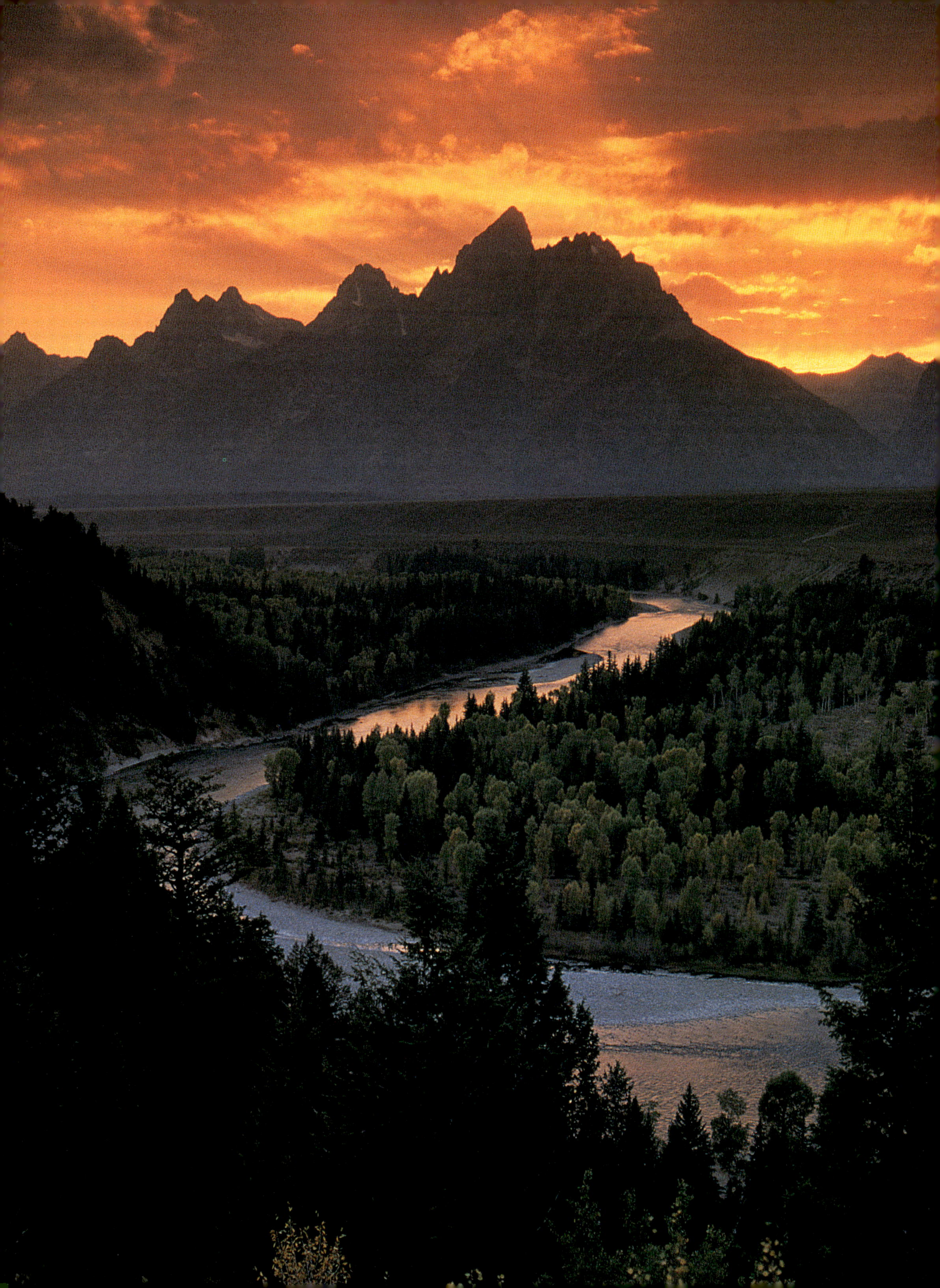

had been almost trapped out and clothing fashions were changing. They would no longer send out supplies; it would not be worth the money or time.

It seems fitting that Jesuit missionary priest, Pierre Jean De Smet, was present at the final rendezvous in 1840. The Bible would follow the tracks of the explorers and trappers, leading the way for the settlers. The trappers had no intention of settling in the wilderness; they had hoped to make sufficient money from beaver pelts to retire rich men east of the Mississippi River. John Colter did return to Missouri in 1810, but when he died three years later of jaundice, his estate was valued at less than $230.

Naming and Claiming

With the passing of the trappers, the era of permanent settlement began in the West, though for a few years homesteaders bypassed the Rockies and Jackson Hole. It was deemed inhospitable to farmers. Former trappers, like Jim Bridger, Kit Carson, and Thomas Fitzpatrick, found new employment for their skills, guiding the wagon trains to Oregon and California on the trails they had found.

The explorers and trappers left a legacy of place names in Jackson Hole. Although the Indians knew the Teton Range as Teewinot and the Hoary Headed Fathers, the trappers initially called them the Pilot Knobs because the three peaks were visible from such great distances. A French-speaking guide or trapper on the west side of the range must have been feeling nostalgic, when he described them as "Les Trois Tetons," or Three Breasts. Once the name was etched onto Bonneville's map in 1837, the Tetons they were and would remain. Teewinot was attached to a peak northeast of the Grand Teton and which is part of the Cathedral Group.

Legend has it that trapper William Sublette in 1829 named the valley for David "Davey" Jackson, who had hunted in the Hole for many years and was employed by the same company as Sublette. Whatever the truth, by 1837 Jackson's Hole–a hole designating a deep valley in trapper parlance–appeared on maps of the area, differentiating it from Pierre's Hole on the west side of the Tetons.

John Colter's name has been memorialized in a bay on Jackson Lake and in a canyon on the west side of the same lake, both in Grand Teton National Park. The Bridger-Teton National Forest commemorates mountain man Jim Bridger and the Jedediah Smith Wilderness remembers his more reverent compadre. The 1872 Hayden Expedition honored Beaver Dick and his wife, by naming two of the most beautiful lakes beneath the Tetons, Leigh and Jenny.

In *Journal of a Trapper, or Nine Years in the Rocky Mountains, 1834-1843*, Osborne Russell wrote of Jackson Hole: "The great altitude of this place, however, connected with the cold descending from the mountains at night, I think would be a serious obstruction to the growth of most kinds of cultivated grains." Russell may have been correct, but his assessment did not deter people from migrating to the valley.

Four decades passed after the last of the trappers before bachelors turned homesteaders and became the valley's first long-term residents. In 1883, John Carnes and John Holland began building sod-roofed cabins in The Swamp, an inviting name for the marshy area near Flat Creek, land that is now the National Elk Refuge. Although Carnes and Holland dug irrigation ditches to water their hayfields, by the mid-1890s the two men and their families had moved on–to Idaho and Oregon. But others were already taking their places, and many more would follow.

The Mormon Clan

The summer of 1889, the Oregon-bound Mormon clan of Sylvester Wilson detoured to St. Anthony, Idaho, where the extended family was swayed by Elijah "Uncle Nick" Wilson's story of the hay to be mown in Jackson Hole. Six years later, Uncle Nick, Sylvester's brother, homesteaded present-day Wilson, but remains famous to children across the U.S. for his memoir, *The White Indian Boy.* This classic tale captured the imaginations of thousands of youngsters. After all, who hasn't thought of running away to live with Indians? Anything to avoid boring farm chores. For two years during the 1850s, the adolescent Uncle Nick lived with Chief Washakie's Shoshones, before returning to his family in Utah. His adventures continued as a rider with the Pony Express in 1860, and later as a scout for the U.S. army–all before he turned back to the mundane task of farming. Uncle Nick's less stirring tale of Jackson Hole's provender turned out to be true enough, and the descendants of Sylvester Wilson and Selar Cheney today must number in the hundreds.

Ervin and Mary Jane Wilson, Spring Gulch rancher Joyce Imeson Lucas' grandparents, were among Bishop Wilson's flock who pushed and pulled wagons over Teton Pass in November of 1889. "My grandmother with a six-week-old baby? Can you imagine?" says an incredulous Joyce. "It took them two weeks. They had brought a few head of milk cows, but they didn't make it [to spring]. Those old pioneers, they didn't have anything." Her husband, Rod Lucas, interjects: "Except plenty of game."

With winter upon them, the Wilsons and Cheneys had to wait until 1890 to homestead South Park. That first full year, the families organized a school, and by 1895 Uinta County, of which Jackson Hole was then a part, deemed South Park a school district. The land those first Mormons homesteaded begins near the present-day Jackson Hole High School and stretches almost as far as the South Park Bridge over the Snake River. Although large sections of their hayfields have been subdivided into housing developments, such as Rafter J and Cottonwood Park, ranchers between the highway and the Snake still put up hay for cattle and horses.

Rod Lucas's father, Lee, came into the country on horseback in 1896 to hunt. It started to snow and Lucas never made it back to Nebraska; he homesteaded the following year along what became Spring Gulch Road. In 1906, Lucas married Eva Phillips. Rod was born in 1918 in a log cabin which is now part of the garage shed behind the two-story, 1928 vintage frame house in which he and Joyce live. "This house was one of the mansions [in Jackson Hole]," he said. "We had a 32-volt electric system. There was a generator in the basement, and it used to run two or three times a week." It was the 1950s before electricity reached Spring Gulch Road. Although their house is only six miles from Jackson, Lucas said it took an hour to get there by horse during the summer–if it was not mud season–and up to two hours in the winter.

OUTFITTERS

For as long as people have been settling here, they have been hunting and trapping these animals, or guiding visitors to hunt or watch the big game. Read the stories of those first homesteaders and you realize it was tough to get through a winter on what could be grown in a garden or raised on the hoof on 160 acres. Sooner or later, many of them turned to guiding and outfitting for wealthy easterners, and opening up dude ranches to cater to that clientele; that source of cash income for residents has not changed.

Today about forty licensed outfitters and guides operate out of Jackson Hole. They provide a variety of services, from hunting to horsepacking, in Grand Teton and Yellowstone national parks and on the Bridger-Teton National Forest. College students from as far away as Maine and sons and daughters from Moran to Hoback have ended up guiding and outfitting in the valley, sharing their love and knowledge of this place's nooks and crannies. These days, they have to consider ecology and history as they lead clients on hunts with cameras as frequently as with rifles. Without guides and outfitters, many folks would never have the chance to see these wild animals or the places they inhabit, and they would never understand why they have been preserved.

Pre-med student and alpine skier Paul Gilroy arrived from Lake Forest, Illinois, in 1962, hiring on first with Betty Woolsey at Trail Creek Ranch west of Wilson. Over the years, he performed the Jackson Hole job shuffle: wrangling horses and shoveling snow on ranches, pounding nails, working as a camphand, and even getting on with the film crew for a television series, *The Monroes*, while it was shot in the valley. For eleven years, he also operated a float trip company, finally selling out to Barker & Ewing in 1974.

His resume sounds like that of many migrants since the opening of the Jackson Hole Ski Area in 1965: working to ski, skiing to work; leaving as the season required to find jobs or to play. Somewhere along the line he became a businessman with 100 horses, a sleigh ride concession, a dozen employees, and apartments to rent. "I've created a monster," he said with a smile. "You hate to see opportunities go unanswered."

He mixes entrepreneurial spirit with his knowledge of the outdoors. "I come from a long line of hunters," he said. "My grandfather was a market hunter. My father was a schoolteacher, but when not in school, we were hunting or fishing. My mother was in the horse business all of her life."

Before establishing his own hunting camps down the Hoback River on the southern border of Jackson Hole and another up the Buffalo Fork at the north end of the valley, Gilroy worked for, or took over camps from, oldtimers like Albert Feuz and Holly Leek, Stephen Leek's son. Between Gilroy's two current camps, he averages almost sixty hunters in a season for elk, deer, antelope, moose, big horn sheep, and black bear.

What gets to him today is paperwork and lack of hunting permits. "They've put a limit on the number of people I can take in the summer time. None of this improves the service to my clientele, nor does it benefit the environment."

"Jackson's a popular destination," explained Fred Herbel. "There's more diversity of species here than in Casper, where it's mainly deer and antelope. And…there's the world's largest elk herd. That's a calling card." Herbel's path to Jackson Hole crosses Gilroy's. Beginning in 1963, the Wyoming native worked as a wrangler at the White Grass Ranch, a once-popular dude ranch at the base of the Tetons. "It was a beautiful job. All I did was take pack trips," he recalls. Those ten-day outings were spent in the Gros Ventres, the Teton Wilderness, and up Berry Creek. Herbel, like Gilroy, served in Vietnam, returning to the White Grass for the 1969 and 1970 seasons. Like Gilroy, he knows this country.

Herbel explains the number of hunting licenses and the seasons are determined each year by such factors as habitat, carrying capacity, and human tolerance. "The trick is how to do that," he said. "[Then] the problem is getting the hunters to the elk that we want harvested. You take your best shot and Mother Nature throws in her two cents. Then, you throw in the bio-politics." Everyone, from hunters and outfitters to environmentalists and government biologists, lets everyone else know how best to manage the wildlife.

Facing page: Pack train heads for high country adventure in Jackson Hole. ERWIN AND PEGGY BAUER

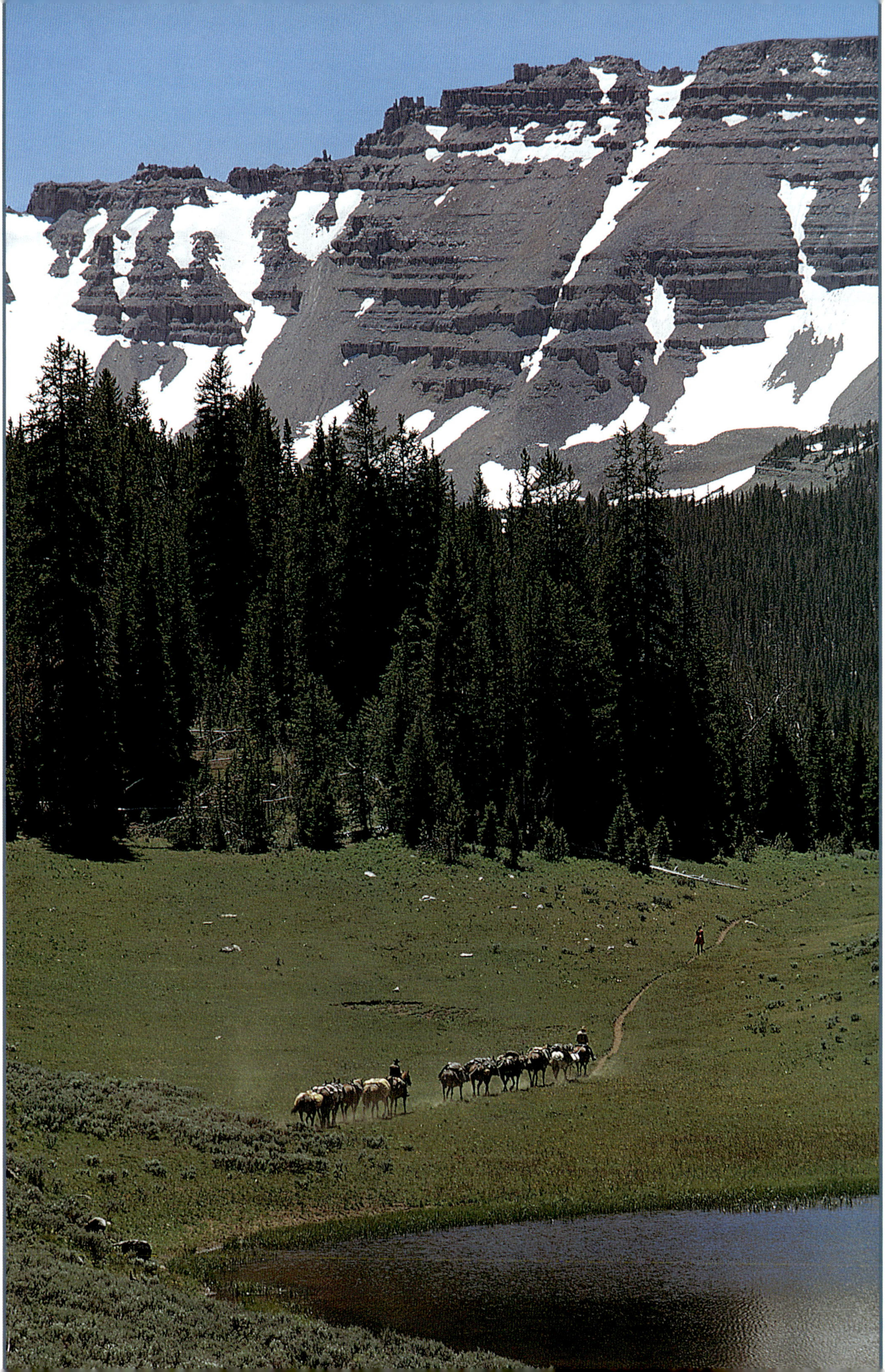

"The whole valley was mostly Mormons until after the war [World War II]," said Crystal Nethercott. A Baptist Church was built in 1912, while the original St. John's Episcopal Church was started in 1916, the same year that the Episcopalians started building a hospital.

Today, almost twenty Christian denominations are active in the valley, and Jewish holidays are celebrated as well. Adherents of Eastern religious beliefs and practitioners of pagan rituals also are represented within the community.

Growing Up

By the 1890s people were building cabins from one end of Jackson Hole to the other: up country in Buffalo Valley and down to the junction of the Hoback and Snake rivers. In 1896, the James May and the James Budge families were the first to cross the Snake River in pursuit of land north of the Gros Ventre River between Blacktail Butte and Kelly. Although not all of those homesteaders were Mormons, the area with its straight avenue bordered by farms and fields came to be called Mormon Row.

Thomas Alma Moulton had established a claim in the same area in 1907, and by 1912 had permanently moved to the property with his bride, Lucille, and young son, Clark. The following year, Moulton began building a barn, adding on as agricultural needs arose, and finally finishing it in the 1930s. Moulton's barn on Mormon Row must be the most photographed structure in Jackson Hole, sitting as it does in a grassy field with the Grand Teton watching over its shoulder. Any national magazine or newspaper article, whether assessing preservation or tourist amenities, inevitably features a picture of the barn, its log and planed wood surfaces golden at sunrise, an emblem speaking to the stamina of the early homesteaders.

A decade after the first Mormon Row settlers, William Kelly built a sawmill closer to the Gros Ventre Mountains in the area that would become the town of Kelly. The Kelly Post Office opened in 1914. Today, Kelly, like Wilson with Hungry Jack's General Store and Nora's Fish Creek Inn, retains much of its rural quaintness.

In 1925, however, Kelly's population and commercial activity almost warranted designation as the seat of government for the newly created Teton County. Before that and following Wyoming statehood in 1890, Jackson Hole was part of Uinta County, with the county seat 190 miles away in Evanston. By 1913, Jackson Hole was part of Lincoln County.

Modern Scene

Jackson became the Teton County seat instead of Kelly, which is now enclosed in Grand Teton National Park. Teton County is a 2,873-square-mile domain stretching from the Snake River Canyon just south of Hoback Junction, north almost to West Yellowstone, Montana. In between, the county embraces all of Jackson Hole, Grand Teton National Park, and the Teton Range, portions of Targhee and Teton national forests, and a sizeable chunk of Yellowstone National Park, including Yellowstone Lake and Old Faithful. Although the county encloses approximately 2,300,000 acres, only three percent, or 75,000 acres, are in private hands and therefore taxable. For the most part, the public lands are under the jurisdiction of federal agencies, a situation typical of much of the West.

Jackson is the only incorporated town in Teton County. The communities of Moran, Kelly, Moose, Wilson, Teton Village, and Hoback Junction, are all Postal Service addresses, and most of them serve their communities with at least a general store. During the 1980s, *Outside* magazine designated Wilson's zip code, 83014, as trendy, noting it is home to "designer ranches." Moran, Kelly, and Wilson operate elementary schools. Students in the smaller communities, once they enter upper grades, attend Middle School and Jackson Hole High School near Cottonwood Park in Jackson.

With her 1897 purchase of land from John Simpson, Grace Miller provided for the town of Jackson. While her husband, banker Robert Miller, gained a local reputation as a hay merchant, Grace gained national attention when she became the first mayor of an all-woman town council in 1920. The town of 350 was living up to the Wyoming standard of recognizing women's rights. On December 10, 1869, the Wyoming Territory had become the first governing body in the union to give women suffrage–probably less because it believed in equal rights, and more because it hoped to pad the sparse electorate. The first order of business for the distaff council: collect unpaid taxes and establish financial accountability.

The community had a public meeting place as early as 1897 when the Clubhouse, also known as the Gun Club, was erected on the east side of the present-day Town Square. Yet the first hotel, the Crabtree, was not opened until 1907. More recently, the Crabtree housed a mountaineering shop until undergoing rehabilitation. Today, it houses a real estate office. Jackson Mercantile, run by the Van Vleck Brothers, opened in 1918, and Jackson Hole Hardware in 1923. Those businesses, like others that catered to a more rural community, disappeared long ago from the Town Square, replaced by dozens of retail enterprises that market arts and crafts, household accoutrements, and clothing. Jackson Drug on the corner of Cache and Deloney, offers a special treat in Jackson's central business district: a soda fountain.

It was not until 1914 that the valley got its first financial institution when Jackson State Bank (JSB) opened near the Town Square. The ubiquitous Robert Miller–he also headed up the Teton National Forest when it was created in 1908–oversaw the bank's startup with $10,000 in capital. In 1981, the United Bank Corporation of Wyoming purchased the bank's assets of $57 million. By the end of September 1995, Jackson State had added a branch near the "Y" and at The Aspens on Teton Village Road, and its assets had grown to $260 million.

Today, two other banks are in business. Key Bank on Pearl Street took over the coffers of the former First Wyoming Bank and is part of a national chain. The Bank of Jackson Hole, the newest lender, also has expanded beyond its Powderhorn Mall location to a drive-up at The Aspens.

Five years before Grace Miller set aside land for a town, the first post office in the valley was located at Marysvale, just north of Jackson. Early post offices were moved from home to home, business to business; some of the towns that they served no longer exist, such as Zenith and Grosvont.

DIANA STRATTON

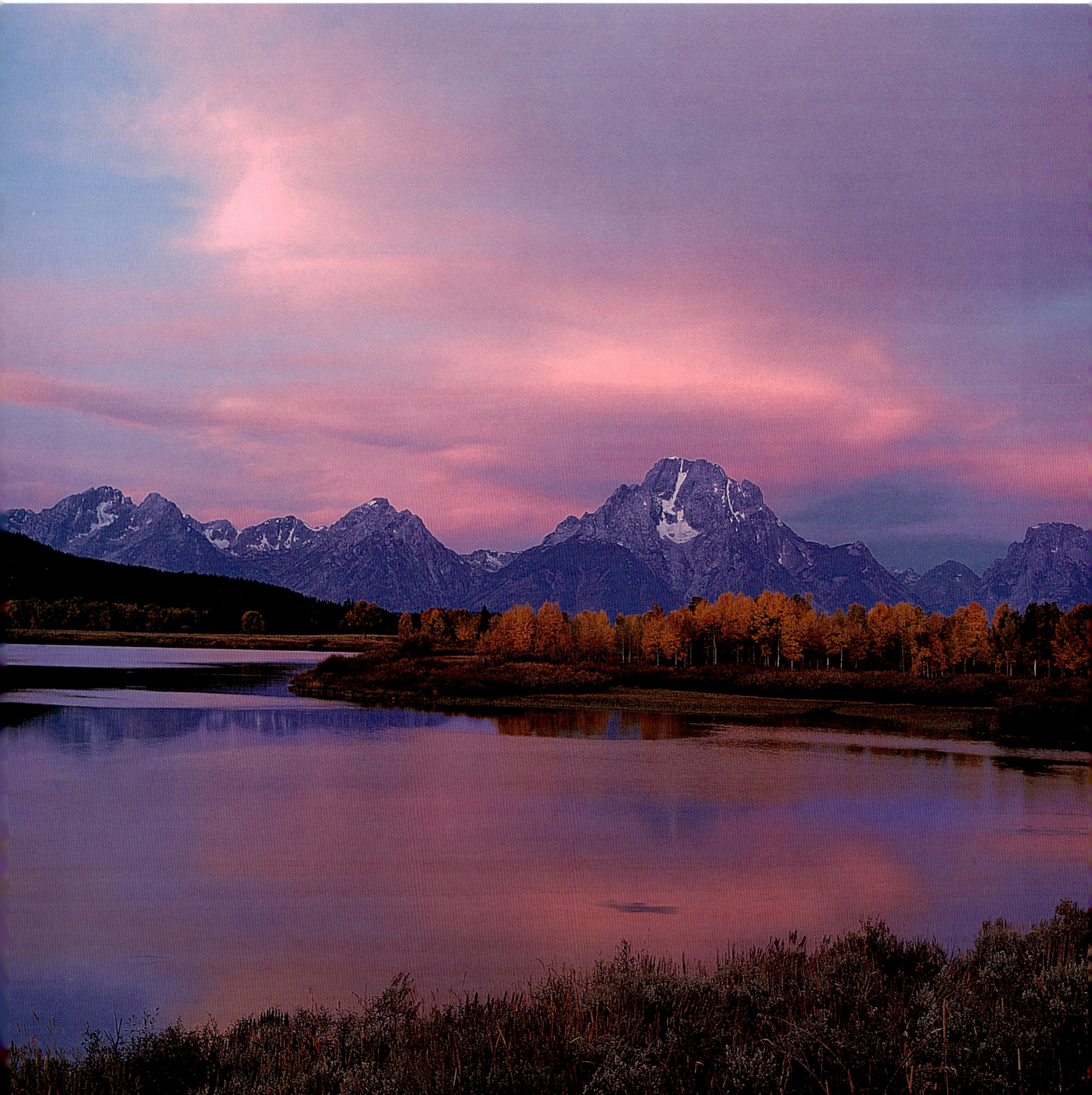

Predawn light in autumn on serene Oxbow Bend in Grand Teton National Park.

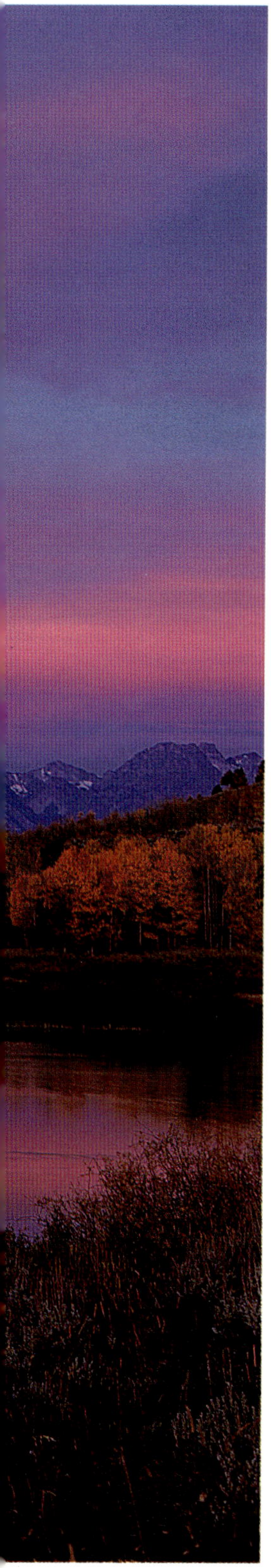

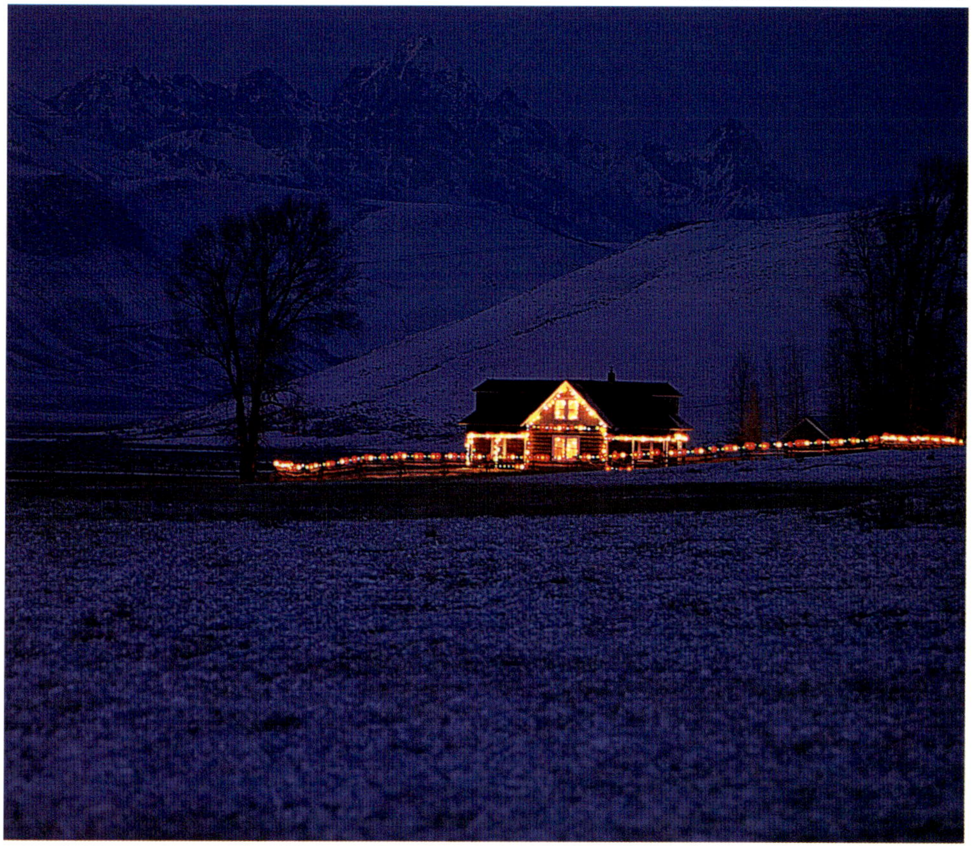

STEVE WANKE/BORLAND STOCK PHOTO

Holiday lights around the home of a ranger on the National Elk Refuge.

Nowadays, nearly everyone has to go to town–Moran, Moose, Kelly, Wilson, Teton Village or Jackson–to pick up their mail. That makes each post office gossip-central. In 1995, Jackson added a second zip code and a 25,000-square-foot main post office on Maple Way, a noticeable increase from the old 6,000-square-foot structure on Pearl Street.

Before the town of Jackson was incorporated in 1914, newshounds were keeping track of the valley's controversies and community events. The first newspaper, *The Jackson's Hole Courier*, started in 1909 and has long since disappeared. The *Jackson Hole Guide* and the *Jackson Hole News* have added daily editions to their traditional weekly fare. Three local radio stations, public radio broadcasts from the University of Wyoming, and a local television station are other media in the region.

Among stories told by those who were born before the 1960s, the advent of television in their lives remains especially vivid. Roger Millward's story seems authentically Jackson Hole. Sometime after 1954 when the very first television broadcast was made in Wyoming, Millward and a group of kids sat themselves in a snowbank on Deloney Street and stared at a flickering image through a store window. "It'd be twenty below zero," he said. "We couldn't hear the sound."

The first traffic light was hung on a wire diagonally across Cache Street and Broadway in the early 1960s, and Millward remembers that historic event, too. "Everybody went down and looked at it," he said. At least five additional traffic signals have been installed in Jackson since 1983.

In the late 1960s, Price Millward started Jackson Hole Transportation Company, running the first bus service between the airport and Teton Village. While that private company still operates, the South Teton Area Rapid Transit system, START, was begun in 1984, primarily to get skiers from Jackson to the Jackson Hole Ski Area. The Town of Jackson now administers START's thirty-five runs, which include a route north to the National Museum of Wildlife Art and the National Elk Refuge sleigh ride. People get around the valley as well by one of a handful of taxi companies; many of the resorts and motels also offer bus or chauffeur service to and from the airport and ski areas.

The valley's first doctor, C.W. Huff, opened his practice in 1913 and that meant families no longer had to take the critically sick over Teton Pass to Eagle Rock, now Idaho Falls, or to Sugar City, near Rexburg, Idaho.

St. John's Hospital, by 1960, had moved into a new facility near the Elk Refuge, and in the 1970s added a twelve-bed nursing home. In 1991, the hospital moved into a still-larger facility, a 100,000-square-foot structure built next to the one constructed in the 1960s. Forty-eight nursing home beds were added in the Living Center.

Tourists account for about twenty-five percent of the hospital's patient load. Skiers twist knees, climbers fall off mountains, or motorists slide off a road or into each other, and require emergency transportation to the hospital. Orthopedic surgeons, internists, and physical and massage therapists are among specialists available to treat the injured and ill. Services of alternative health practitioners, including chiropractors and acupuncturists, also are available in Jackson.

Since the 1980s, Jackson Hole has seen the completion or beginning construction of other modern public facilities. These include the Town Hall with its clock tower, roads maintenance buildings, additional Teton County offices, a trash transfer station, the Pathways system for bikers and walkers, a joint town-county recycling center, and the middle school complex near Cottonwood Park subdivision.

Distances separating Jackson Hole's communities–between South Park and Spring Gulch, between Wilson and Kelly–do not seem far with today's automobiles, paved roads, and snow plowing. The early settlers had to deal with dirt roads and anxious crossings of the Snake River. Bill Menor put in a ferry at Moose in 1892, but sometimes charged a greater toll than his passengers wanted to pay.

A bridge over the Snake River near Wilson made travel easier, but it was not erected until 1915 and soon washed out. A more substantial structure opened in 1922. After World War II, the Wyoming Highway Department realigned the road between Jackson and Wilson, and built another bridge farther downstream. During the winter or when an accident occurs on the state highway, though, the Snake River can become a moat between the West Bank and the rest of the valley; for that reason, a second bridge closer to Teton Village has been proposed.

Construction of a new highway between Wilson and Victor, Idaho began in 1968. It was to have included a bridge at the base of Glory Slide which engineers hoped would provide room for avalanches to slide under and thereby allow automobile traffic even in winter. However, the nearly completed bridge was twisted beyond repair in January of 1970 when a monster avalanche let loose.

Law and Order

On any day during the summer, the population of Jackson Hole swells to that of small city. That influx of people, intent on recreation or seasonal work, has meant the development of public services, including law enforcement and medical care, necessary for a city of 50,000 people. The valley has never been a paradise free of crime before the tourists came. Mysterious murders and vigilante actions, armed robberies and white-collar crime have followed the course of settlement. Deadman's Bar on the Snake River got its name after three German gold prospectors were found brutally murdered there in 1886. One member of the same party, John Tonnar, was charged with the murders but he pleaded self-defense and was released. The Cunningham Cabin, now on the National Register of Historic Places, can be visited in Grand Teton National Park. It's the site of an 1893 posse's ambush and killing of two men rumored to be horse thieves.

Sheriff Roger Millward said most felonies in Teton County these days involve property and not crimes against people. "The sheer volume has gone up," he said. Since 1974, the sheriff's office has grown from seven employees to sixty-five. Because of the extensive outdoor recreational opportunities, from climbing and backpacking to hunting and kayaking, the sheriff's office finds itself performing more searches and rescues than most comparably sized communities. Millward personally has been involved in at least 1,000 rescues.

The search and rescue team is composed of thirty-two people, who have experience digging people out of avalanches, pulling them out of rivers, and getting them to the hospital; the Park also has its team of rangers who regularly rappel from cliff and helicopter to snatch climbers from harm's way. In addition, fire departments in Jackson, Wilson, Moran and Hoback Junction are staffed by volunteers and administered by the county to answer less remote emergencies, lessening the sense of isolation and vulnerability.

GLENN VAN NIMWEGEN

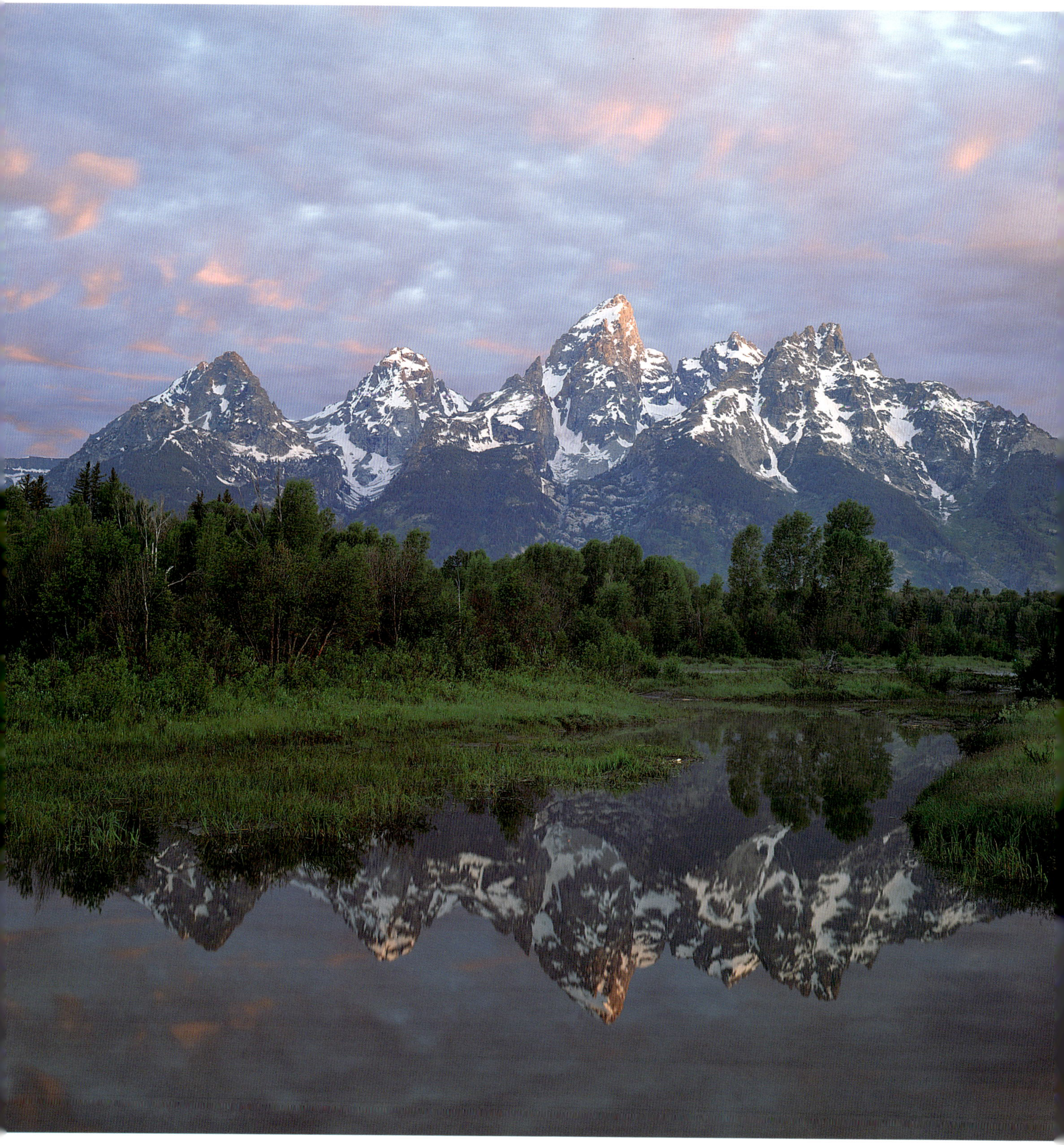

Sunrise on the Tetons reflected in a side channel of the Snake River.

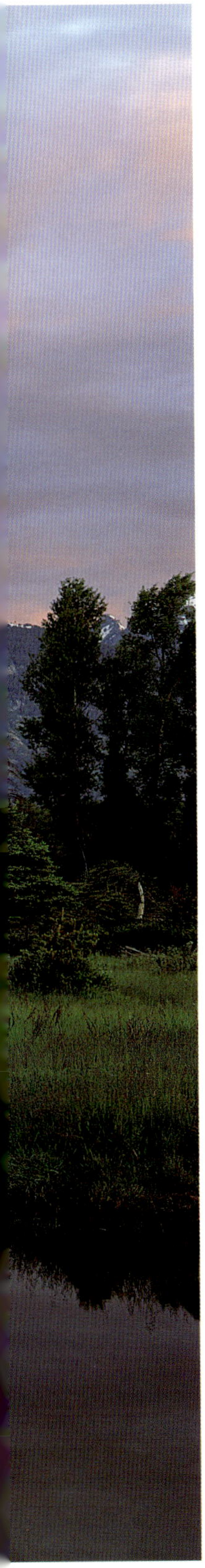

CHAPTER THREE

THE PARK: PAST AND PRESENT

For naturalist-turned-public affairs officer Linda Olson, Grand Teton National Park has always been much more exciting than its sister park, Yellowstone, to the north. "There's the human element," she said, alluding to conflicting personalities and issues that have surrounded the park since its inception. In the 1920s, people were arguing the merits of preserving so much *land* in a park and, in the 1990s, people were arguing the merits of operating an *airport* in such a park.

Impetus for establishing the park was the thought that Jackson Hole is a place needing protection. Before the turn of the 20th century, the United States Geological Survey, which explored the Teton area in 1872, recommended it for inclusion in Yellowstone National Park. The federal and state governments took the first step in overseeing the valley in 1897 when Congress created a National Forest Reserve and expanded its boundaries in 1902. By 1905, the Wyoming Legislature set aside 570,000 acres north of Moran as the Teton Game Reserve to protect migrating elk. In 1908, the Teton National Forest was established, administered by the Department of Agriculture.

The Debate Begins

The effort to preserve Jackson Hole began in earnest in 1916 when National Park Service Director Stephen Mather and his assistant, Horace Albright, toured the area. One look at the Tetons and the pair decided the valley should be part of Yellowstone National Park. In early July of 1918, Albright had become superintendent of Yellowstone and tried to convince Jackson Holers that a park was a good idea. In response, he heard that dude ranchers such as Struthers Burt and cattle ranchers were adamantly opposed to the establishment of the park for economic reasons. According to Robert Betts in his book, *Along the Ramparts of the Tetons,* the dude ranchers feared the loss of the frontier atmosphere that attracted easterners to the valley, and the cattle ranchers feared loss of grazing rights.

Those who have studied the history of Grand Teton National Park and Jackson Hole say opposition to the orginal concept of a park had little to do with what the opponents thought of a forest reserve or of a game reserve in and of themselves. They thought more about what such developments would mean to their livelihoods. The same concerns prevail today among the park's adjacent landowners and those who make their livings more indirectly from the land and from development of the park.

"Gateway communities have a proprietary feeling that the parks are theirs and, therefore, they should have a big piece of what goes on," said Linda Olson, park spokeswoman. She cautions, however, that parks have a national importance that reaches beyond local interests. Wyoming Senator Frank Mondrell, sponsor of an early 20th century piece of federal legislation to extend Yellowstone's boundaries south, recognized that it was not in his interests to continue to promote it and withdrew the bill.

But, regardless of debates in Congress and elsewhere, a land market grew in Jackson Hole attributable to favorable economic conditions and growing awareness of the region's attractiveness. Despite the dude ranchers' hopes of damming a flood of tourists, the tourists came and locals decided to cash in on them by building cabins and gas stations as close as possible to the Tetons. At the same time, beef prices dropped and cattle ranchers lost money and had to borrow from the bank. With or without a park, the demographics were beginning to change.

By 1923, the community also had changed its mind about the proposed national park. An historic meeting was held that July at Maud Noble's cabin north of Moose. From that meeting, developed tentatively Struthers Burt's idea for a "museum on the hoof," but the plan never gathered any financial backing.

Turning Point

Another significant turning point for proponents of the park came during the summer of 1926, when Albright chauffeured the wealthy John D. Rockefeller, Jr. family around Jackson Hole. The sight of tacky tourist facilities set against the backdrop of the Tetons catalyzed Rockefeller into buying the land to prevent further desecration. There are reports that Rockefeller's wife was especially appalled by what she described as "all that junk," apparently referring to the hastily constructed tourist accommodations smack in front of the Tetons. One can surmise that Albright, Yellowstone Park superintendent, knew exactly what he was doing when he brought Rockefeller to Jackson Hole. It seemed to be the perfect partnership: a bureaucrat who knew what he wanted but had no financial resources, and a businessman with enormous resources captivated by a vision. By 1927, Rockefeller's Snake River Land Company was buying the land.

With support from the Wyoming congressional delegation, the bill that established Grand Teton National Park was passed in 1929 and signed by President Calvin Coolidge. The original park boundaries, however, only protected the mountains and the adjacent piedmont lakes, such as Jenny and Bradley lakes, and did not include Jackson Lake. One of the new park's first orders of business: remove the offending tourist buildings.

People in Jackson Hole continued to be concerned about loss of grazing land, hunting rights, and tax revenues resulting from the establishment of the park and Rockefeller's acquisition of substantial tracts of land through the Snake River Land Company. For fourteen years, beginning in 1929, park-related issues were hotly debated in Congress, in the Wyoming capitol and in Jackson Hole. Loss of economic and political power was feared by Jackson Hole residents. Westerners have traditionally exhibited fear of too much government, and that fear became mixed in this Wyoming valley with apprehension about the actions of wealthy easterners and the loss of grazing land, hunting rights, and tax revenue. Yet Albright and Rockefeller remained dissatisfied with the size of the park. By 1933, the Snake River Land Company had bought or had options to buy approximately 35,000 acres. It was a time of severe economic depression nationwide, and many ranchers gladly relinquished their holdings to a party with money enough to acquire them.

FDR Gets a Message

The war of words continued between 1929 and 1943. In 1934, Wyoming Senator Robert D. Carey introduced a bill in Congress to extend the original boundaries of the park, but it got nowhere. The debate had expanded to include concerns about who would control the elk herd. Concern grew over reports that Rockefeller interests intended to sell their holdings in Jackson Hole, about 32,000 acres, unless the federal government accepted the land as part of a federal preserve. Secretary of the Interior Harold Ickes carried that message to President Franklin Roosevelt. Finally, in 1943, in the middle of World War II, Roosevelt signed legislation establishing the Jackson Hole Monument, which preserved 200,000 acres of the valley. "It wasn't like Roosevelt didn't have anything better to do than to do something about this area," said one long-time Jackson Hole resident who has studied the park's history. But, the debate continued for the next seven years, including at least two congressional attempts to abolish the new Monument. Hearings were conducted, countless speeches given, editorials published, even vigilante action taken. In all the fervent argument, the state of Wyoming was squared off against the federal government, Congress confronted the Department of the Interior, and local residents often found themselves at odds with one another. By the end of the decade, the various parties were tired of bickering.

Wyoming Senators Joseph O'Mahoney and Lester Hunt, who formerly had opposed the Monument, finally worked out a compromise with the National Park Service. In 1950, President Harry Truman signed a bill creating an expanded Grand Teton National Park. Among other things, the compromise guaranteed Teton County reimbursement for loss of tax revenue from property included in the park. Additionally, hunters would be deputized to be allowed to hunt in the park, ranchers would keep grazing leases during their lifetimes, and the federal and state governments would jointly manage the elk herd. Of Teton County's 1,840,000 acres today, approximately 75,000 acres are privately held or are in conservation easements.

Another park-related controversy continues over the location of the Jackson Hole Airport within the park. When Price Millward started building hangars and clearing brush for runways six miles north of Jackson in the 1950s, he could not have anticipated the furor that his airfield would stir in decades to come. Millward worked for General Steel in Utah during World War II, then returned to Jackson Hole and began flying from a field near The Virginian Lodge. By the 1950s, he had outgrown that site and was buying land and working with Jackson and Teton County officials to clear an airstrip at the current site of the Jackson Hole Airport. Because of its location within

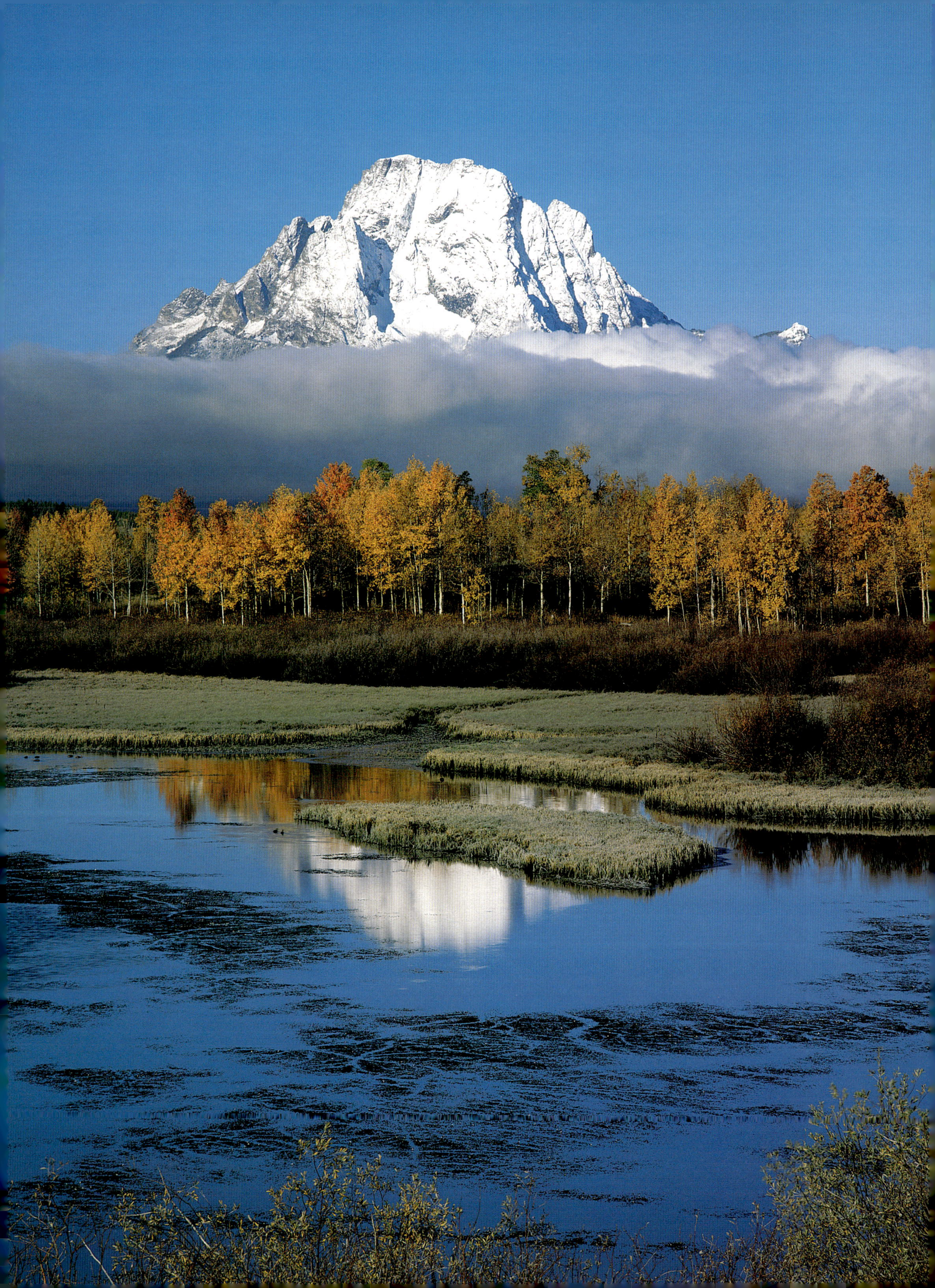

DIANA STRATTON

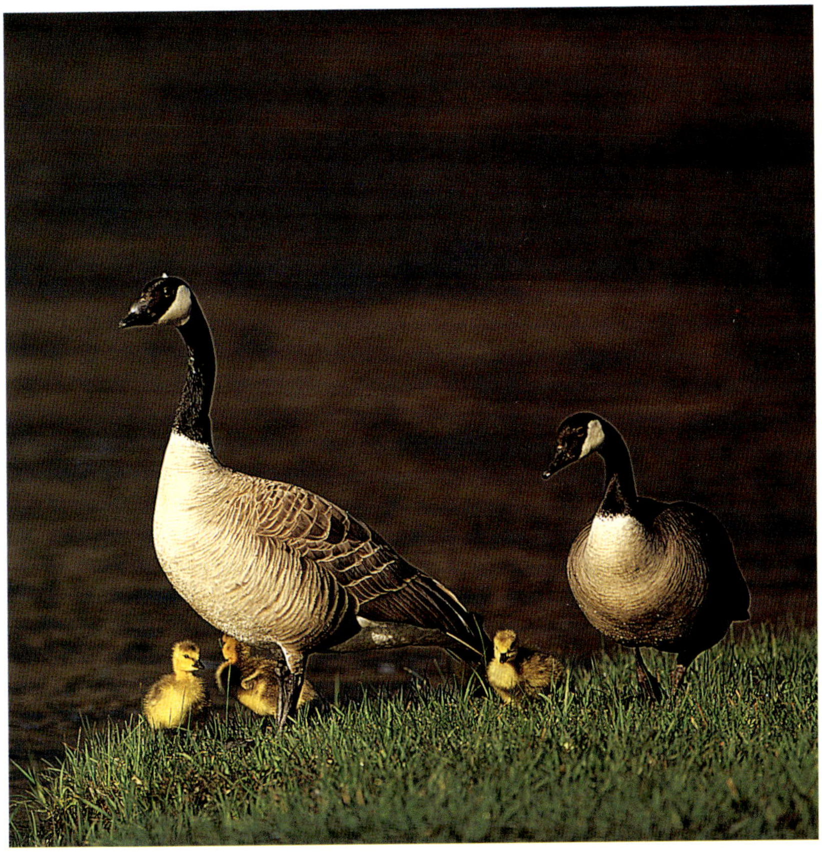

Left: Pair of Canada geese and goslings by the Snake River.

Below: Bank fishing along the Snake River in the park.

Facing page: Mount Moran from Oxbow Bend. GLENN VAN NIMWEGEN

JAMES BLANK

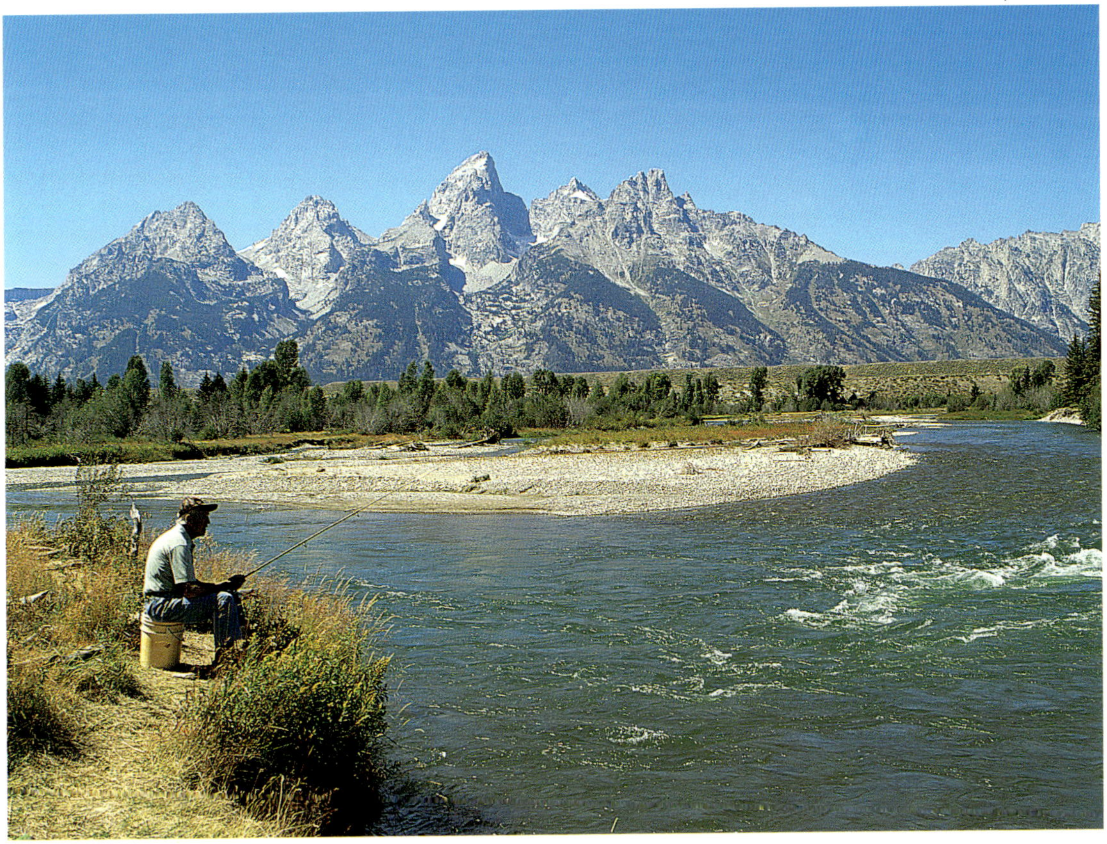

Grand Teton National Park, some people want the airport dismantled and moved, while others want its runways lengthened and facilities improved for safety reasons.

Controversy aside, the park has preserved about 485 square miles of habitat that would not be preserved if it weren't for Horace Albright's drive to tackle a problem. In 1972, the John D. Rockefeller Jr. Memorial Parkway that connects Yellowstone and Grand Teton national parks also was established.

Within the park, ownership of about 1,000 acres is mixed between the federal government and private parties. For example, the park holds Triangle X Guest Ranch in fee simple, but it is operated with a special use permit by the Turner family as a concessionaire.

Park Pleasures

The National Park Service unavoidably creates, and deals with, conflict of a different kind. The NPS has a mission to protect natural resources and provide for public enjoyment of those resources. Linda Olson, spokeswoman, said, "Resource protection and enjoyment by the public of that resource don't always mesh." Publicizing Grand Teton National Park and improving its services–from campgrounds to programs–as well as services in gateway communities such as Jackson Hole have encouraged greater and greater numbers of people to come. As early as 1938, Fritiof Fryxell was predicting that "inevitably" the visitors to the park would increase beyond the "tens of thousands" of his era; in the 1990s, the numbers surpassed Fryxell's expectations, pushing into several million.

When non-winter tourists come, Grand Teton National Park offers them scores of amenities, in addition to viewing mountains and wildlife. Some of the five campgrounds–Colter Bay, Jenny Lake, Signal Mountain, Gros Ventre and Lizard Creek–feature trailer hookups, dumping stations, and campfire interpretive programs. Beds and meals also can be found at Colter Bay's cabins, and at Jackson Lake Lodge, Jenny Lake Lodge and Signal Mountain Lodge.

A suggestion for the athletic day-hiker: the breakfast buffet at Jenny Lake Lodge can be a nutritious and delicious start to hiking Indian Paintbrush Divide loop trail. But if that trail seems too little or too much, or if an overnight backpack trip is on the agenda, the park boasts another 180 miles of maintained trails. The twenty-miler up Indian Paintbrush Canyon to Solitude Lake and down Cascade Canyon may be excessive for some, and challenging with an ice ax for most. But from Jenny Lake Lodge or the nearby String Lake parking lot, there are several alternative and easier routes: a walk around Jenny Lake or strolling north to String Lake and Leigh Lake. For a multinight backpacker, Alaska Basin on the west side of the Teton Range would be a worthy destination. The Craighead brothers searched the Alaska Basin for specimens described in their book, *Rocky Mountain Wildflowers.*

To keep the walking to a minimum and the scenery to a maximum, there is the tour boat ride across Jenny Lake providing an exceptional view of the Cathedral Group of the Tetons. From the boat dock on the west shore, it is less than a mile to Hidden Falls and Inspiration Point, two of the more popular viewpoints in the park. Many of the park's trails can also be traveled by horse, and stables are located at Colter Bay, Jackson Lake Lodge, and Jenny Lake.

For the vista-lover, the drive to the top of Signal Mountain on the east side of Jackson Lake is recommended. From its summit, the visitor gets a sense of what makes our valley a Hole with its relatively flat expanse rimmed by mountains. In the fall, Signal Mountain also provides an ideal seat for listening to bugling elk.

In addition to tour boats on Jenny and Jackson lakes, people can enjoy the water of the park's lakes and the Snake River under their own power in canoes, rubber rafts, and kayaks, or by motorized boats, if permitted. Several companies also offer scenic float trips through the seemingly placid waters of the Snake River. Stalwart aquatic sorts can try their arms and legs at windsurfing and waterskiing, but a wetsuit will make bone-chilling Jackson Lake tolerable in August.

While many of the shoulders along the park's roads have been widened, bicyclists need to ride defensively and with a wary eye for side mirrors. Locals relish the short couple of weeks each spring when the road between Cottonwood Creek and Signal Mountain is first cleared of snow and open only to cyclists, walkers, and in-line skaters.

Winter in the park holds its own attractions: cross-country skiing and snowshoeing from Cottonwood to Bradley, Taggart and Jenny lakes; ice fishing on Jackson Lake; and snowmobiling on Jackson Lake and along designated roads. In addition to cross-country ski and snowmobile tour guides, dogsled operators are available for those unfamiliar with the terrain. During this season, lodging is limited within the park, so motel reservations in Jackson are advisable.

The Visitor Center at Moose and another at Colter Bay that feature Native American artifacts are good places to begin any stay in Grand Teton National Park. While the park, like Yellowstone to the north, generally remains open from early May through mid-November, visitors should call the Moose Visitor Center at 307-739-3300 for the most current information.

DAVE G. HOUSER

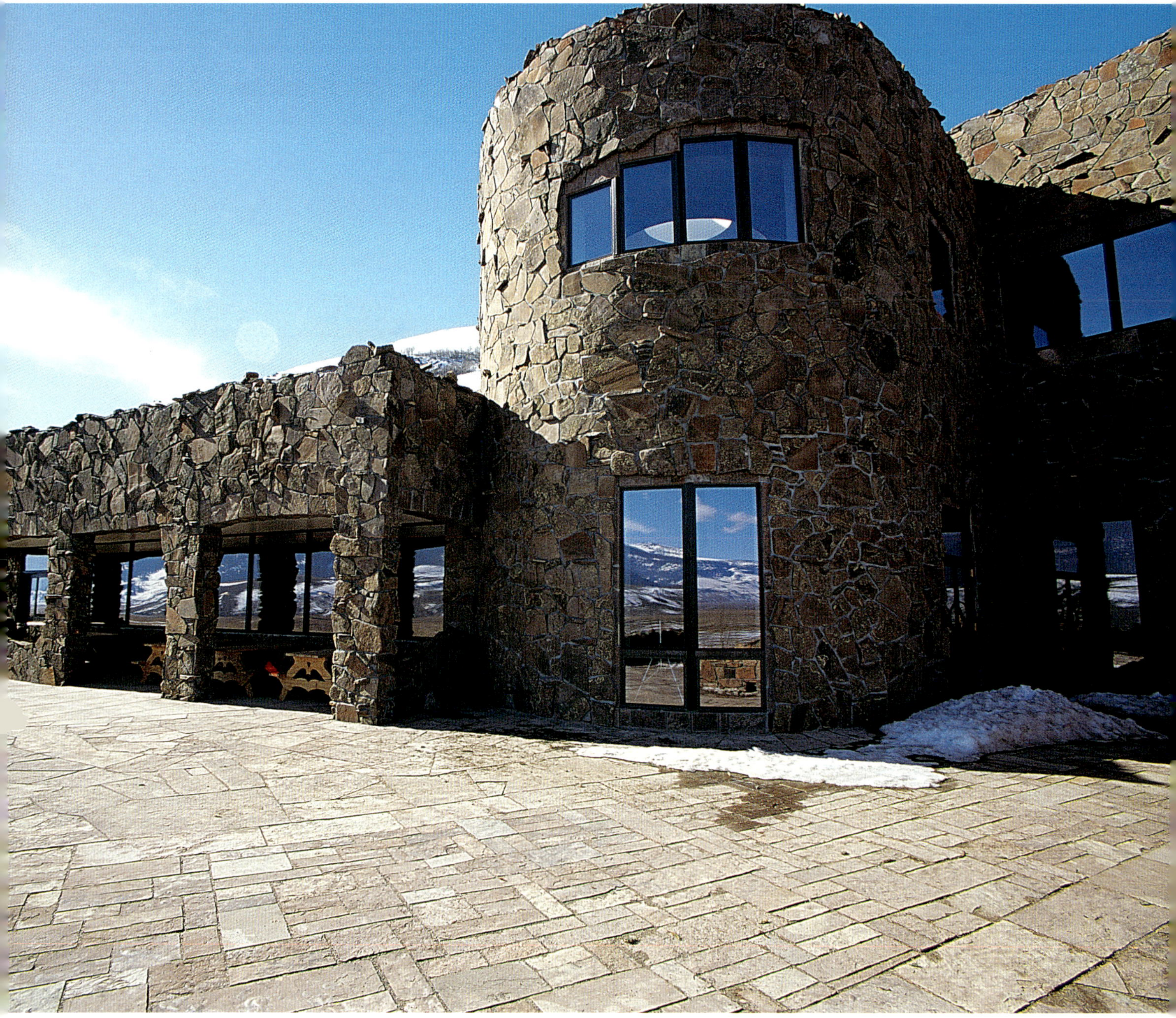

The National Museum of Wildlife Art opened its new building north of Jackson in 1994.

CHAPTER FOUR

THE CULTURAL SCENE

As trappers and settlers migrated to and through this valley, so artists have come, drawn by the call of visual, performing and literary muses. Depending on the season and the year, you can expect to find the Mormon Tabernacle Choir singing at Walk Festival Hall, a dance company under a tent on Snow King Mountain, a first-run movie at one of three theaters, a zydeco band at the Mangy Moose Saloon, an art opening at one of two dozen galleries, or a reading by the likes of Ivan Doig at the county library.

William Henry Jackson is credited with the first photographic rendering of the Tetons. To obtain his 1872 photographs of the mountains, Jackson spent nine days hauling an oversized camera and developing equipment on mules to the top of Table Mountain on the western edge of the range. The resulting fine-grained photograph of the Grand Teton and her lesser sisters made his effort to reach such a dizzying perch worthwhile.

The painter Thomas Moran accompanied Jackson a year earlier on another project for the United States Geological Survey. Alongside Jackson's photographs, Moran's watercolors and oils of the Yellowstone area inspired easterners and Congress to establish the first national park. Although Moran never traveled into Jackson Hole, his name was affixed to Mount Moran, the hulking mountain at the north end of the Teton range which is reflected dramatically in Jackson Lake and the Oxbow of the Snake River.

Between those first expedition artists and today's residents, few people documented their passage through the Hole, either in pictures or in words. A few haunting images survive, though, images that speak to the early settlers' desire to have culture in the wilderness. In a 1910 photograph, Edith Sargent plays a violin beneath the shade of a canopy, a gramophone her only accompaniment, the Tetons and Jackson Lake a hazy backdrop beneath a summer's sunset.

Painters

Beginning in the 1930s, painters began trickling in and, after World War II, word spread that the Tetons provided incomparable vistas to paint. By the 1950s, Conrad Schwiering was operating a gallery and, with J. Paul Bransom and Grant "Tiny" Hagen, offered summer art workshops. By the late 1960s, with western art sales booming, more artists were coming to paint and to stay.

Others took longer to transplant their studios and personal galleries to Jackson Hole. A native of Devon, England, landscape and historical painter Roy Kerswill first came in 1948 on a canoe trip and returned to live in 1960. Before settling here in 1970, John Clymer worked for many years as an illustrator in New York City. Painter Joanne Hennes began her courtship in 1954, finally settling here in 1976. "Mountains have so many different moods," Hennes explains as the reason for her move. "The Tetons are especially perfect. The Tetons are always different."

Beginning in the 1950s, galleries representing nationally-esteemed artists opened, and though the number thinned out somewhat in the early 1990s, new galleries appear each season. Trailside Americana has been in business the longest, having moved into the old B&W Market on the Town Square in 1964.

No longer just a stop on the Western art stage, Jackson Hole has become home to artists using anything from photo realism to abstraction to imbue their work with nostalgia, humor, and political commentary. Although sculpture and paintings depicting the West of trappers and explorers, cowboys and Indians dominate the gallery art scene, some resident painters and mixed media artists create works as wild as anything found in Los Angeles or New York. All of which does not mean that most can give up day jobs as school teachers and dish washers.

The variety of galleries and artists has encouraged Jackson to become the venue for national events and institutions. In 1985, the Chamber of Commerce organized the first Jackson Hole Fall Arts Festival, an effort to attract tourists to the community from mid-September through early October when the weather is unpredictable and the snow has yet to cover the slopes. The Arts Festival has shortened the off-season, and is held in conjunction with the National Arts For The Parks competition, gallery and studio tours, "Quilting in the Tetons," and theatrical offerings.

Wildlife Art

Few communities of Jackson's size can claim an institution of the caliber of the National Museum of Wildlife Art. As curator Maria Hajec said, "This is not just about wildlife art, it's about all art. Much of the art is about the expansion of the West, and that has changed through time. For that reason, Teton County–typifying the changing demographics of similar communities around the West–seems a fitting place for such a museum.

The motorist traveling the highway north out of Jackson toward Grand Teton and Yellowstone national parks has to look twice to discern the museum on the flank of East Gros Ventre Butte. The color and stone design of the 51,000-square-foot building form it naturally, almost invisibly, to the hillside. The structure evokes a rock outcropping or a crumbling ruin in the process of rejoining the land. Museum Director Dan Provo said of the architecture: "The building continued to evolve in response to people's comments. We had our concepts and we added the community's to the mix."

The museum collection began in 1987 with 250 pieces of art and was housed in three galleries in a former office building on Town Square. By 1994, when the new facility opened with 2,000 pieces and access to traveling exhibits, the museum filled a dozen galleries, featuring the works of Carl Rungius, Conrad Schwiering, Charles Russell, and Ken Carlson. In its first year at the new location, 140,000 people went through the doors.

Much of the museum's focus, beyond pure art conservation, is on education and outreach. Since 1988 the museum has developed programs for children, beginning with 100 Teton County grade schoolers, increasing to 5,600 participants from a four-state region in six years. Because the museum has two classrooms and an auditorium, it also provides a setting for conferences and symposia which make use of its collections.

The museum lies directly west of the 25,000-acre National Elk Refuge with its thousands of wintering elk as well as deer, coyotes, ravens, geese, swans, and raptors in seasonal residence. It is an ideal locale for joint cultural and natural history projects. "Here's a museum sitting on a ridge from which you can literally see a whole variety of animals represented in the collection," said Provo. The Museum has conserved thirty-five of its seventy acres in scenic easements for use by students in its programs.

Photographers and filmmakers also have been among the visual artists placing their stamp on–and being stamped by–the landscape and by the animals and people who inhabit this place. They have explored meadows and roads here and in exotic corners of the world, and brought their still and moving images to our screens and bookstores. In recognition of the valley's scenery, Jackson Hole has hosted special film and photography events: the Photography at the Summit, the Banff (Canada) Festival of Mountain Films, and the Jackson-based International Wildlife Film Festival.

Throughout the years, grassroots organizations and events have sprung up in response to perceived cultural needs within the community. As Georgie Morgan recalls, the Teton County Library was "the earliest cultural center in Jackson Hole." An art show was held each summer on the library lawn during the 1950s until it outgrew that location and moved to the high school.

The impulse to provide an outlet for arts and crafts, as well as an income for local artists and crafts workers, has grown into the juried Mountain Artists Rendezvous, held twice each summer–in mid-July and again in mid-August–and attracts artisans and buyers from around the country. The Art Association also sponsors a Christmas Bazaar the first weekend in December.

Morgan was instrumental in the establishment of the Jackson Hole Art Association. The association initially grew from a campaign to bring arts education to elementary and secondary schools, Morgan said. Potters Larry and Pam McCool, and jeweler Sharon Rudd taught the arts to students and adults alike. For more than three decades the Association has offered a variety of art workshops. In 1965, the Art Association put on the valley's first contemporary art show.

Performers, Writers

Dance music by local musicians has always enjoyed support in the valley. At least two generations of dance-goers rode horses or drove wagons or sleighs to dance halls

DAVE G. HOUSER

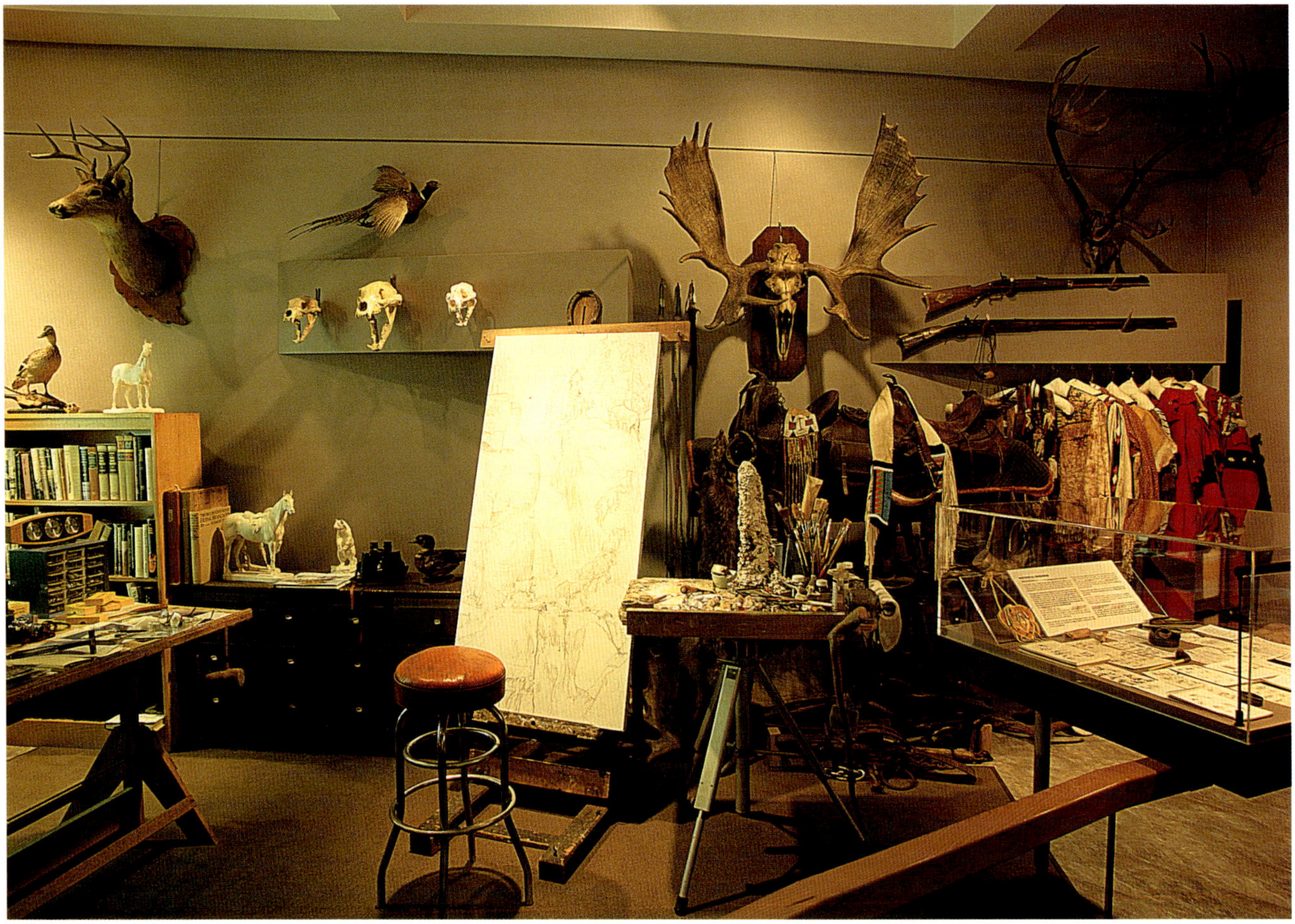

DAVE G. HOUSER

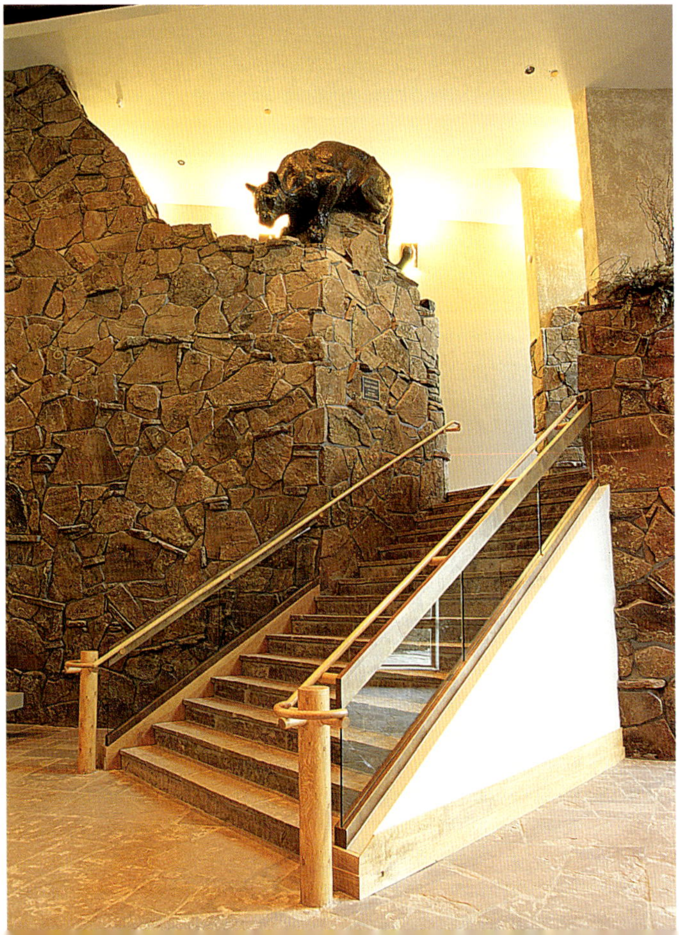

Above: The studio of famed western artist John Clymer is on exhibit at the National Museum of Wildlife Art.

Right: Painstaking efforts to blend with nature succeeded in the design of both the interior and exterior of the National Museum of Wildlife Art.

DAVE G. HOUSER

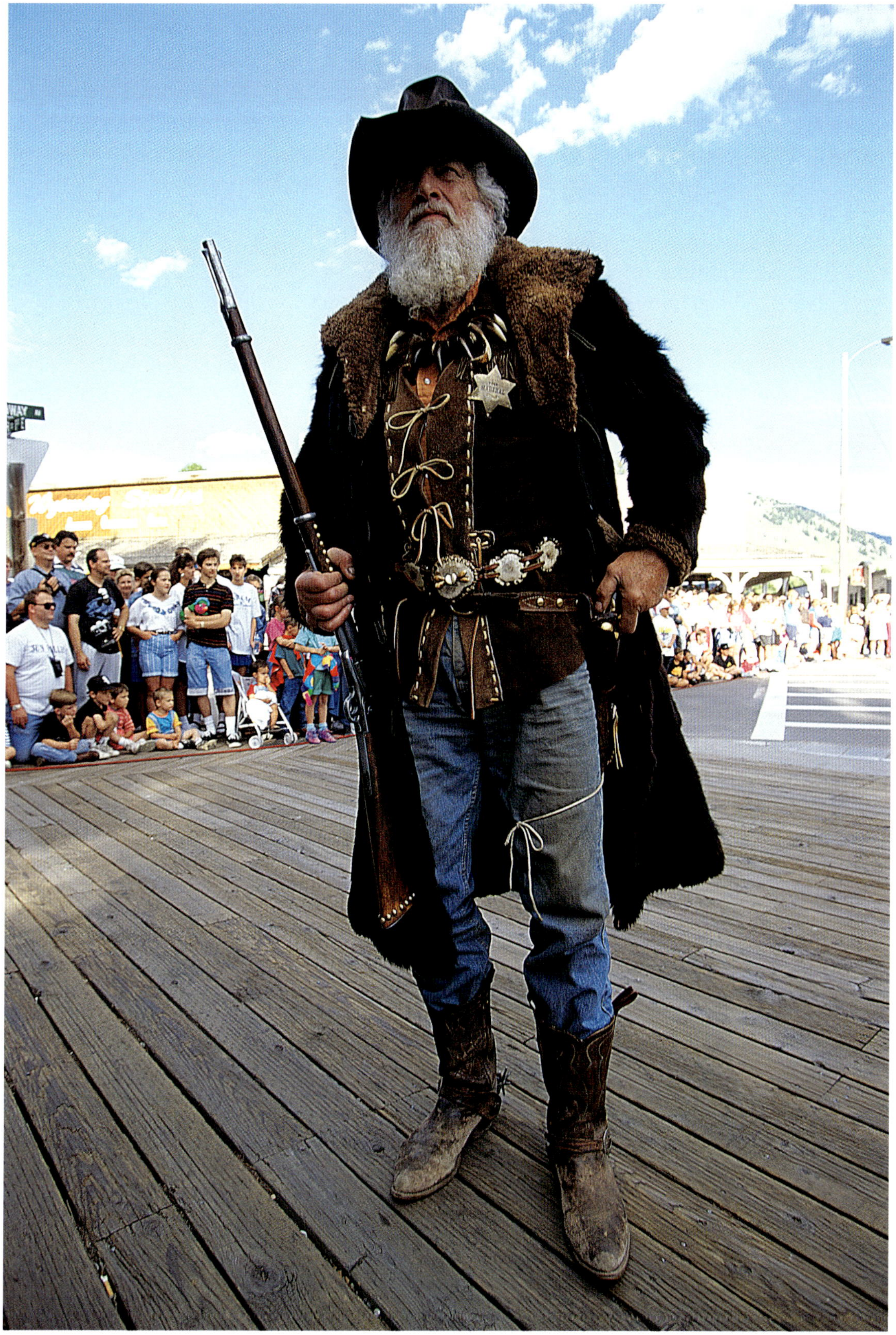

A "town marshal" oversees nightly performances of Town Square Shootout *in Jackson.*

around the valley. If they weren't headed for Ward's across from the Elk Refuge, or the dance hall at Jenny Lake, it was The Jungle in Wilson, where Wesley Bircher served up barbecued beef at the intermission. Bob and Crystal Nethercott, the grandchildren of early homesteaders in Wilson and South Park, remember dancing and roller skating at Bruce Porter's Rainbow, located in Dirty Jack's Theater on Cache Avenue in Jackson. Dance music still thrives in Jackson Hole. Since 5:30 p.m. on Sunday, Feb. 16, 1969, the Stagecoach Band has been cranking out tunes every Sunday at the bar of the same name in Wilson.

The valley is home to a variety of musicians, some with more than a local following. People have looked forward to winter and summer concerts that mark the return of Loose Ties, a bluegrass favorite at festivals around the United States.

To spotlight local acoustical music talent, Dornan's Bar at Moose has regularly sponsored an old-fashioned hootenanny since 1994. The "Hoot," as originator Bill Briggs calls it, harkens to the semi-wild gatherings of the early 1960s when climbing musicians–or was it musical climbers?–sang and sipped "Teton Tea" around a campfire at the south end of Jenny Lake. Dornan's has recreated the "tea"–a concoction of tea and wine, lemon and sugar.

Derrik & the Dynamos is a local rock group featuring guitarist Derrik Hufsmith, son of resident classical composer George Hufsmith. The Larry Hestand Trio plays jazz at a local bistro. And, there's the Community Band, complete with tuba, for just about anyone with an interest in performing.

Big name performers–from Chris LeDoux to The Radiators–come through Jackson Hole regularly, appearing at the Mangy Moose Saloon with its memorabilia, the Cowboy Bar with its saddle barstools, the Teton County Fair, and the Snow King Center.

No place can call itself truly cultured without classical music. The Grand Teton Music Festival, now based at Teton Village's Walk Festival Hall, puts Jackson Hole on the map every summer for eight glorious weeks. The American Bus Association listed the Music Festival as one of the 100 events to attend during 1996 in the United States and Canada. Thirty-some years ago though, the Music Festival made do with, first, a high school gymnasium seating 250 people and then with a tent capable of holding 500 people, but subject to the whims of wind and weather. Walk Festival Hall seats 900 people, who listen to the symphony composed of premier players from major orchestras, and soloists in wide-ranging programs.

Dancers' Workshop has been providing both classes and performances since its start in 1972 by Patty Noel and Nancy Goodman Lee. In 1986 things came full circle: Georgie Morgan's daughter, Lisa, who was a student with Dancers' Workshop in the 1970s, became artistic director. Today, the organization has its own regional touring company, Three Rivers Dance Company, and brings professional dancers to work with students and to perform throughout the year.

The dramatic arts have appeared here in various guises, from national acting companies to dinner theater. Actors Co-op and the Jackson Hole Theater Company have taken to the stage at the Pink Garter, sometimes collaborating with other groups, such as Dancers' Workshop. Summer visitors and residents looking for more traditional western fare find musical comedy at three locales in Jackson, and cowboy music and poetry at the Bar J and the Bar T Five.

Jackson Hole's best known dramatic arts event is the Shoot-Out on the Town Square. Featuring good guys and bad guys, a stagecoach holdup, and a hanging, the Shoot-Out has been going strong six evenings a week since the 1950s. In reality, stagecoaches never traveled our roads, nor was anybody hanged, though a few "bad" guys–sheepherders and suspected horse thieves–were shot up or run out by early vigilantes.

Hollywood-produced western movies have had a prosperous association with Jackson Hole. What better scenery could be captured on celluloid than that "for free" beneath the Tetons? The filmmakers started coming in the 1920s, and have continued migrating to the valley, though these days they primarily make commercials.

Undoubtedly, the most famous of all movies filmed here was *Shane* with Alan Ladd in the early 1950s; no less mythic were *Jubal* with Glenn Ford and *The Big Sky* with Kirk Douglas, made here during the same period. In the minds of many people who saw those and similar films, the Tetons became synonymous with the West, with the rugged individualism and community spirit that living in such places demanded.

Teton County residents are accustomed to seeing celebrities on the street. These days the rich and famous generally maintain a less flamboyant profile than did actor Wallace Beery. In 1943, Beery led an unsuccessful effort to keep the federal government from taking over the newly declared Jackson Hole National Monument.

Writers, as well, have been offering insights on the valley since the early trappers' forays; many of the trappers' journals, including Osborne Russell's written in the 1840s, offer a less than romantic image. Owen Wister's name has long been linked to the valley because of his visits between 1887 and 1912, and his 1902 penning of *The Virginian*, into which some Wyomingites may fantasize themselves as characters.

Today, the writers with Teton County zip codes and license plates offer a wide range of perspectives in the form of screenplays and comic novels, guides on hiking and natural history, and book-length essays on hunting and the machinations of the law. According to the Teton County Library, more than 230 published authors have at times made their homes in the valley.

In 1992, a group of resident writers, including Win Blevins (*Give Your Heart To The Hawks*), Tim Sandlin (*Sex and Sunsets*), and Warren Adler (*War of the Roses*), joined with the University of Wyoming to inaugurate the first Jackson Hole Writers Conference, held each July. Over the years, the literary impulse has found expression through several local magazines and publishing houses, which have produced articles and books extolling a variety of subjects, for example, horses, climbing, community values, and history.

Education

Education in Jackson Hole has not been far behind the arts in spreading beyond its traditional setting and taking root throughout the entire community. As early as 1972, elementary school principal Gary Elliott was organizing community classes to combat

BOB WOODALL

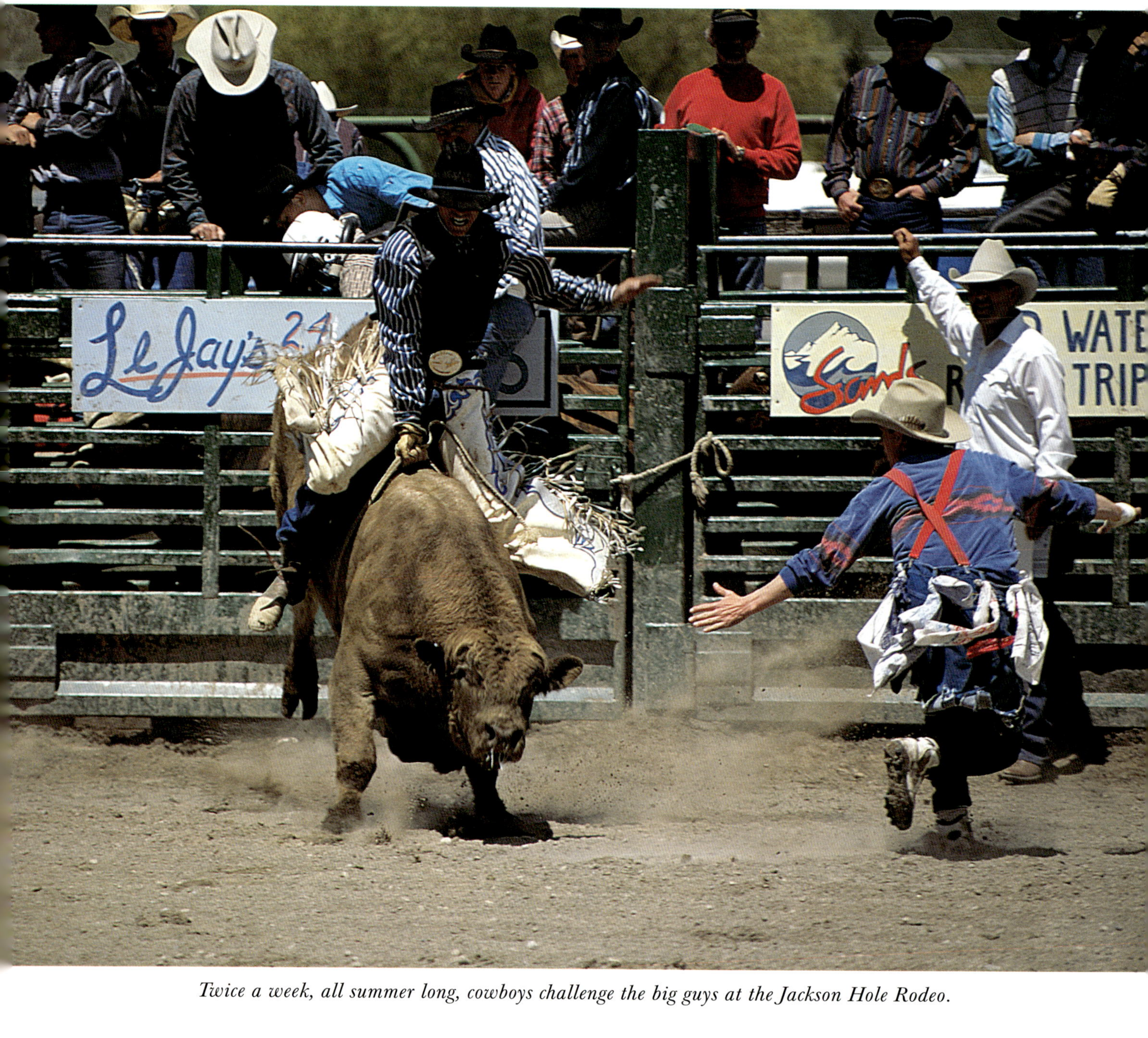

Twice a week, all summer long, cowboys challenge the big guys at the Jackson Hole Rodeo.

JAN BUTCHOFSKY

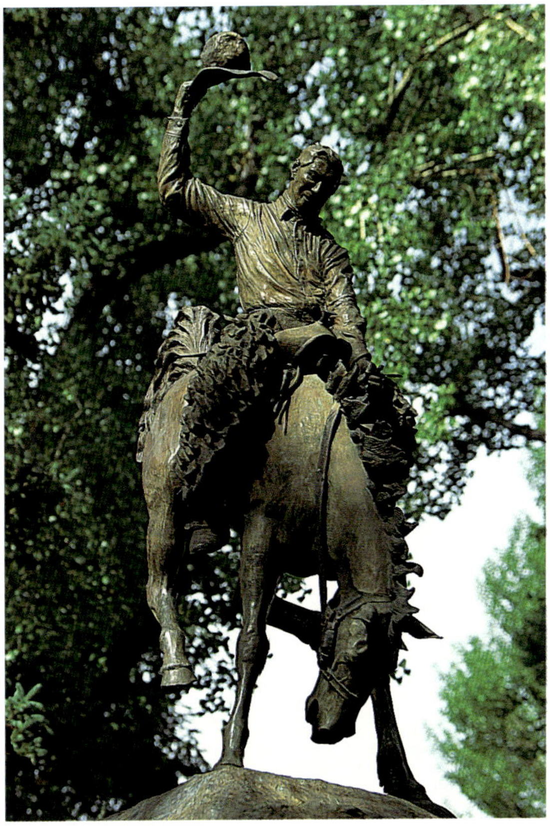

Right: This rodeo cowboy will ride his bronc forever in a Jackson park.

Below: Some long-time residents of Jackson still remember the day the town got its first traffic light.

JAMES BLANK

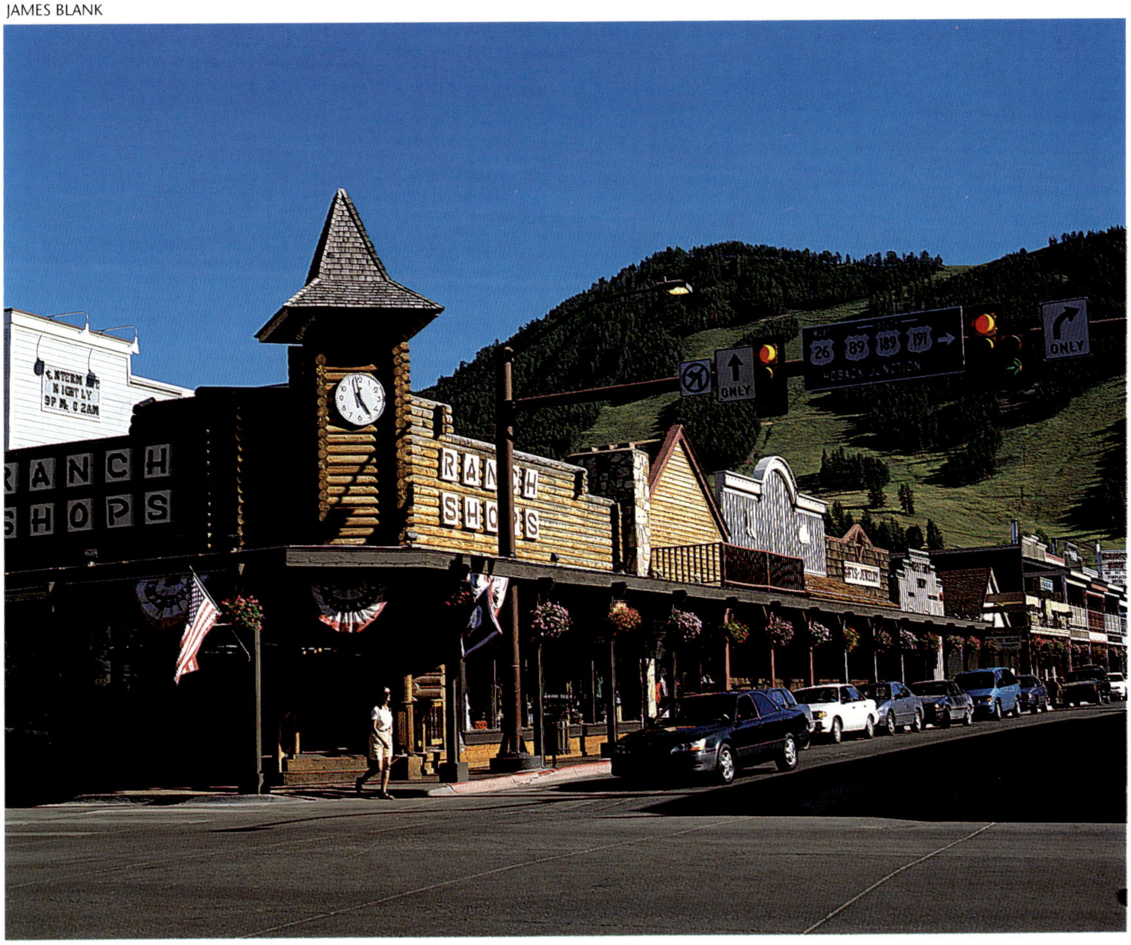

cabin fever and to make use of Teton County School District's facilities. "We only ran a winter session and probably had 30 classes," Elliott recalls. "The most popular was wine-tasting up at Dornan's. But if I had three people interested in Greek, it'd go. The sky was the limit."

Three decades later the result is the Jackson Community Education program, which embraces a broad definition of the word education. Today, the program attracts 250 credit students and 400 non-credit students each semester. According to Community Ed director Mary Gridley, everything from ice cream making and fly fishing to conversational Spanish and animal tracking has been offered over the years.

Since 1980, Central Wyoming College has overseen the programs, and has provided more traditional courses. Because of the presence of St. John's Hospital and a continued demand, both here and nationally, for registered nurses and nursing assistants, Community Ed offers a formal, two-year nursing program and an associate college degree. The University of Wyoming also plays a part in local education. As recently as 1992, the University was flying professors in as part of its School of Extended Studies. Advances in telecommunications make some courses available on compressed video, meaning students sitting in a Jackson classroom interact with the professor lecturing at the same time in Laramie.

For a number of Jackson Holers, the Teton Science School in Grand Teton National Park was their doorway to the valley. As a Utah State University student, Lee Riddell was an environmental education intern at the Teton Science School in 1975. Now, a business she and her husband started has blossomed into Riddell Graphics, an advertising and design firm with its own building and sixteen employees. The first book Lee designed was a collection of Grant Hagen's work, connecting her to the local art tradition.

Georgie Morgan recalls the Science School's tentative beginnings: "We had collected money to start a prep school, but then Ted and Joan Major came along and wanted to have a summer program." Besides the Majors, and Georgie and John Morgan, others who helped launch the school were rancher and journalist Virginia Huidekoper, Olympic skier and dude ranch owner Betty Woolsey, and conservationist Mardy Murie. The summer program became the Teton Science School, which has earned national recognition for its natural science education programs. Arts and philosophy have been integral to the Science School's programs and to its interface with the community. The school's "Art in Nature" series in the 1970s featured Fritjof Capra and Buckminster Fuller.

Since the school's inception in 1967, its annual budget has grown from $12,000 to more than $1 million. The number of students, both youth and adult, has grown, from a handful of Hagen and Morgan and Huidekoper kids in the 1960s to more than 12,000 now. All of them have had access from the Science School's 40-acre campus near Shadow Mountain to thousands of acres of wilderness in the Bridger-Teton National Forest. Again, cooperation among federal and state government agencies and local people and organizations has been important to a local institution's survival and integration with the community.

The variety of educational opportunities available in the valley has lessened residents' sense of isolation over the years, allowing students to complete some portion of their college requirements in their hometown. Although these educational organizations, and others with similar missions such as the Snake River Institute, offer hundreds of classes and workshops each year, ideas of starting a liberal arts or music college continue to surface.

Pam McCool, as director of the Art Center in 1979, was asked by the National Endowment for the Arts to survey funding for the valley's arts groups. She was surprised to learn that Teton County folks were spending more money–through taxes and donations–per capita than all but one other community in the United States. All of which still makes the valley the envy of other cultural groups in Wyoming.

The valley's myriad arts groups prompted the Community Foundation in 1990 to form the Arts Task Force. "We recognized that there was a need to bring the arts together," administrator and consultant Candra Day said. The first action by the Arts Task Force was the creation of the Cultural Council of Jackson Hole, and one of the Council's most visible actions has been the quarterly publication of a calendar of county-wide and regional events. Collaboration is the key word in Day's vocabulary, the essential ingredient in a successful association of arts groups in Jackson, whether that group is Jackson Hole High School and the Science School, or the National Museum and the 4-H Clubs. One project the Council wants to move beyond the dream stage is construction of a community cultural center.

DIANA STRATTON

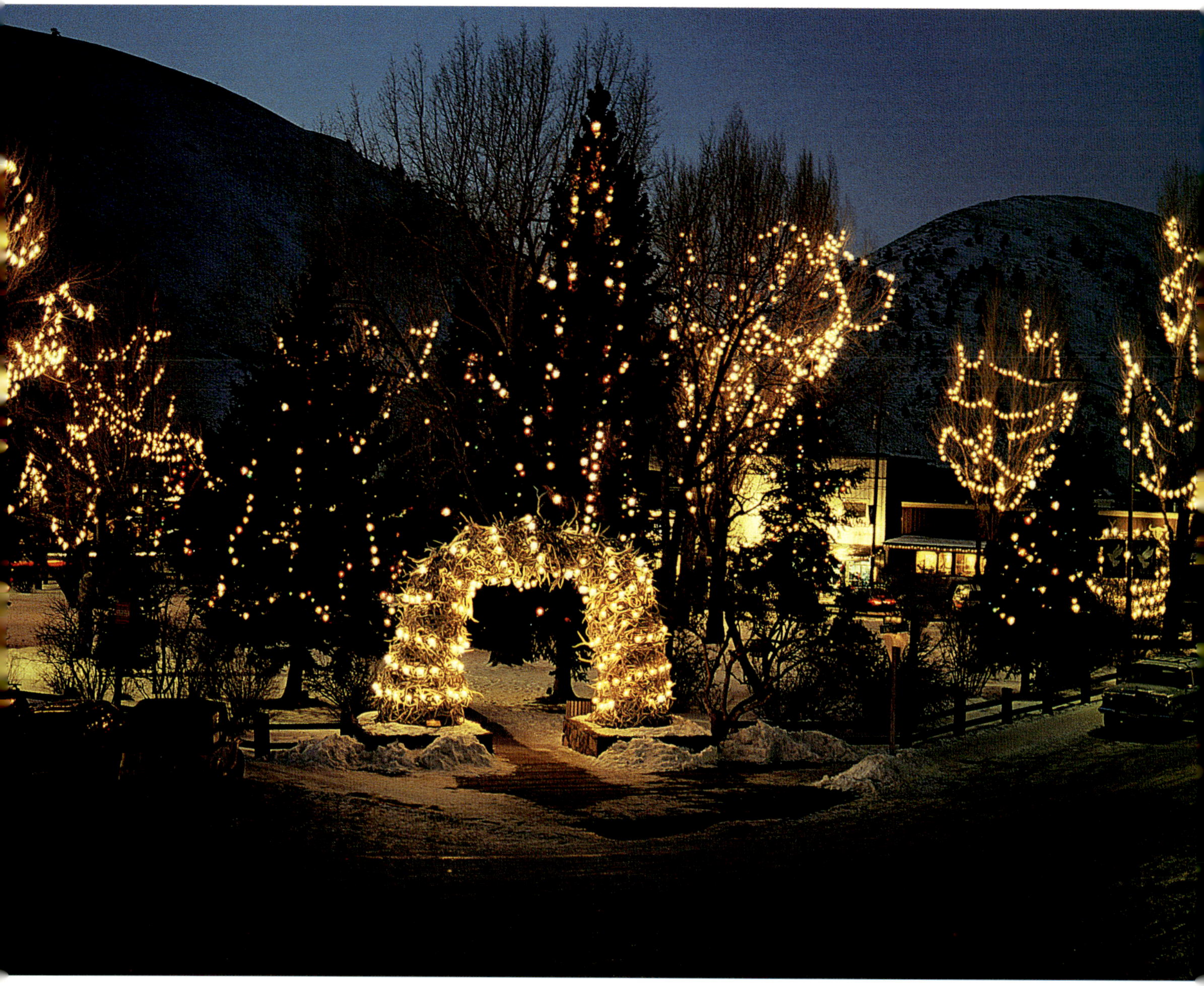

Decorative lights adorn arches of elk antlers and trees in Town Square in Jackson.

CHAPTER FIVE

WESTERN SKI TOWN AND MORE

Tourists visiting dude ranches and Grand Teton and Yellowstone national parks brought Jackson Hole to life in the summers before and after World War II, but winters were times of low-key, homespun fun. That changed in 1965 with the opening of the Jackson Hole Ski Area.

Winter carnivals in the 1930s gave residents something to do and a reason for outside skiers to come to the valley. But the skiing community was not well organized nor was the sport promoted until the advent of the Jackson Hole Ski Club in 1937. The Ski Club began with 23 people and ballooned to as many as 1,600 members. It was as interested in providing social amenities as it was in teaching skiing–from jumping to snowboarding. Just as the passage of animals and plants marked the seasons, so Ski Club events highlighted the winter season's passage for the community: Ski Ball in November, Forty-Niner Ball to break January's monotony, and the Pole-Pedal-Paddle relay in early April.

For almost fifty years the Ski Club's Shelter at the base of Snow King Mountain was home to potlucks and racers sitting out the cold between runs; few cared when the fireplace smoked or that the carpet was a ghastly color. The squat log building, which biologist and conservationist Olaus Murie dedicated in 1944, has been replaced by Snow King Center, with a full-size, indoor skating rink. Although the new public facility provides an athletic venue for youngsters and adults interested in figure skating and rough-and-tumble hockey, the demolition of the old Shelter signaled the end of an era. No longer could dances and box socials alone pay for buildings and coaches.

For three generations, Snow King Mountain has been the town ski hill, and it and the first operator, Neil Rafferty, were valley parents' babysitters of choice. From the 1950s through the 1970s on Snow King's slopes, the Ski Club held Little Waxers races, which encouraged children to develop their skiing prowess and competitive edge. Talk to anyone who grew up in the town hill's shadow during those years and you'll be talking to someone who learned to ski not long after learning to walk. Chances are they could carve perfect turns with two-by-fours attached to their feet. All of which explains why so many of the youngsters who participated in the Ski Club's program earned berths on college and national squads, represented the United States at the Olympics, and coached prestigious alpine and nordic teams.

Making Champions

After winning the 1967 U.S. and Canadian Alpine Championships, second generation Jackson Holer Karen Budge Eaton was the first Jackson Holer to ski beneath an Olympic flame–in 1968 at Grenoble, France, and four years later at Sapporo, Japan. Fellow natives Peter Karns and Martin Hagen knew their alpine turns, but biathlon–nordic skiing combined with target shooting–grabbed their attention; Karns also competed in the 1972 Olympics, and Hagen in the following three Olympics. Although cross-country skier Kelly Milligan was born in Yellowstone National Park in 1961, her family didn't move to Jackson Hole permanently until 1968; eighteen years later, she joined Olympian Hagen in a then-peaceful Sarajevo.

Before Neil Rafferty installed the 2,000-foot cable tow on Snow King in 1939, skiers were just as likely to head for Wilson and Teton Pass. The annual Pouch Trophy, a regional ski competition during the 1930s, featured jumping at Schofield Hill on Fall Creek Road and downhill and slalom races on Mount Glory above Teton Pass. Even in 1945, the Ski Club held Spring Derby Races on the southern faces of Glory, and watched Betty Woolsey, captain of the 1936 Olympic Ski Team, and Virginia Huidekoper, a top regional skier, lose to a Canadian in the slalom.

The 1946 addition of a chair lift on Snow King apparently didn't stop skiers from heading into the mountains on their own power–with a little help from Rafferty. Into the 1950s his jitney, or taxi service, transported skiers from Wilson to the top of Teton Pass, where a small hut kept adults and children warm between rope tows. Roger Millward recalls the 1950s and 1960s: "If you could talk a parent into taking you to Teton Pass, you'd be in seventh heaven."

A Changed Place

Ask people what has changed Jackson Hole the most and half will say, "The Jackson Hole Ski Area." Before the ski area opened in 1965 at Teton Village on the west side of the Snake River, the valley suffered from an "economic depression for three quarters of the year," said Bill Briggs. That winter he become a full-time resident, though he soon moved over to Snow King and started the Great American Ski School. The Ski Area on Rendezvous and Apres Vous mountains, however, meant people could find work two out of four seasons. Its presence also garnered national and international attention for Jackson Hole. The first director of the Ski Area's ski school was Austrian Pepi Stiegler, gold medalist in the 1964 Olympics. Following the 1994 Olympics, U.S. downhill gold medalist Tommy Moe was signed on to promote the ski area.

The Ski Club put on the Junior Nationals, complete with downhill, slalom, jumping and nordic events, in 1963 on Snow King. But it wasn't until 1967, with the availability of Teton Village's more extensive terrain, that the Ski Club could help stage a World Cup slalom and giant slalom race; the Wild West Classic attracted French super skiers Jean-Claude Killy and Annie Famose to our slopes. Eight years later, Jackson Hole hosted a World Cup downhill race. The NCAA championships and tryouts for the U.S. biathlon team also have been held in Jackson Hole.

Today, the valley boasts three lifts and night-skiing at Snow King, and seven lifts and an aerial tram at the Jackson Hole Ski Area; on the west side of the Tetons—outside the Hole—Grand Targhee Ski Resort caters to powder hounds intent on skiing Wyoming mountains. Despite the availability of chairlifts and groomed nordic tracks at several locations, Teton Pass and the mountainous backcountry that surrounds us still continue to lure alpine and telemarking aficionados, snowboarders, snowshoers, and snowmobilers. Friends who hate crowds or who don't want to spend all day getting to untracked powder and corn snow have bought snow machines to get them deep within the Snake River and Gros Ventre ranges.

Strangers heading into unfamiliar mountain areas should first visit a guide service, ski or snowmobile shop, or the National Park and Forest Service information offices rather than risk becoming the subject of a search and rescue. The novice alpine and nordic skier also should have proper gear and even take a lesson or two.

The Real West

Jackson Hole and other resort communities in the "new" West most often are identified with skiing, but for many people, cowboys and rodeo still seem to typify the Old West. Rodeo conjures hot summer afternoons. A wooden arena filled with cheers. American flags and banners snapping. Lariats snaking through dust and heat. Hooves pounding. Bulls and broncs arching well-muscled backs against a blue sky. Cowboys digging in spurs and thighs. Cowgirls leaning with their mounts to negotiate barrels. Cowboys holding on to make the eight-second buzzer. Clowns, like crazed matadors, distracting enraged bulls.

Roger Millward, fulltime sheriff and sometime rodeo pickup man, roped and rode saddle broncs and barebacks during the 1960s. In his mid-20s, though, he gave it up to raise a family. He returned to the arena in 1989, because his sons, Steve and Scott, then fourteen and twenty-one, had taken up the sport and "it was a chance to be with my boys." In 1993, nineteen-year-old Steve was paralyzed in a bull-riding accident at a rodeo in Montana.

"It's hard for me to go there now and see kids getting hurt," Millward says. "At the same time I have something to offer. I can't blame the sport itself [for the accident]. It's never what you expect it to be. You've got to take the cards you're dealt and play them as best you can."

For Millward, the community's response to his son's accident demonstrates the locals' strong commitment to help people, neighbors and strangers alike, when tragedy hits. People wrote letters and phoned during Steve's stay at a Craig, Colorado, hospital, and before he came home, local carpenters remodeled the home to make it wheelchair accessible.

Rodeo arrived in Jackson Hole in the 1920s with cattle ranching and permanent settlement. After World War II, rodeo became a regular happening, most memorably organized by Walt Callahan in an arena behind his Stagecoach Bar in Wilson. In its heyday, the Wilson rodeo was the only thing to do on a Saturday night. Rodeo promoter Bob McConaughy has described those days: "It was very colorful, but definite-

JACK WILLIAMS

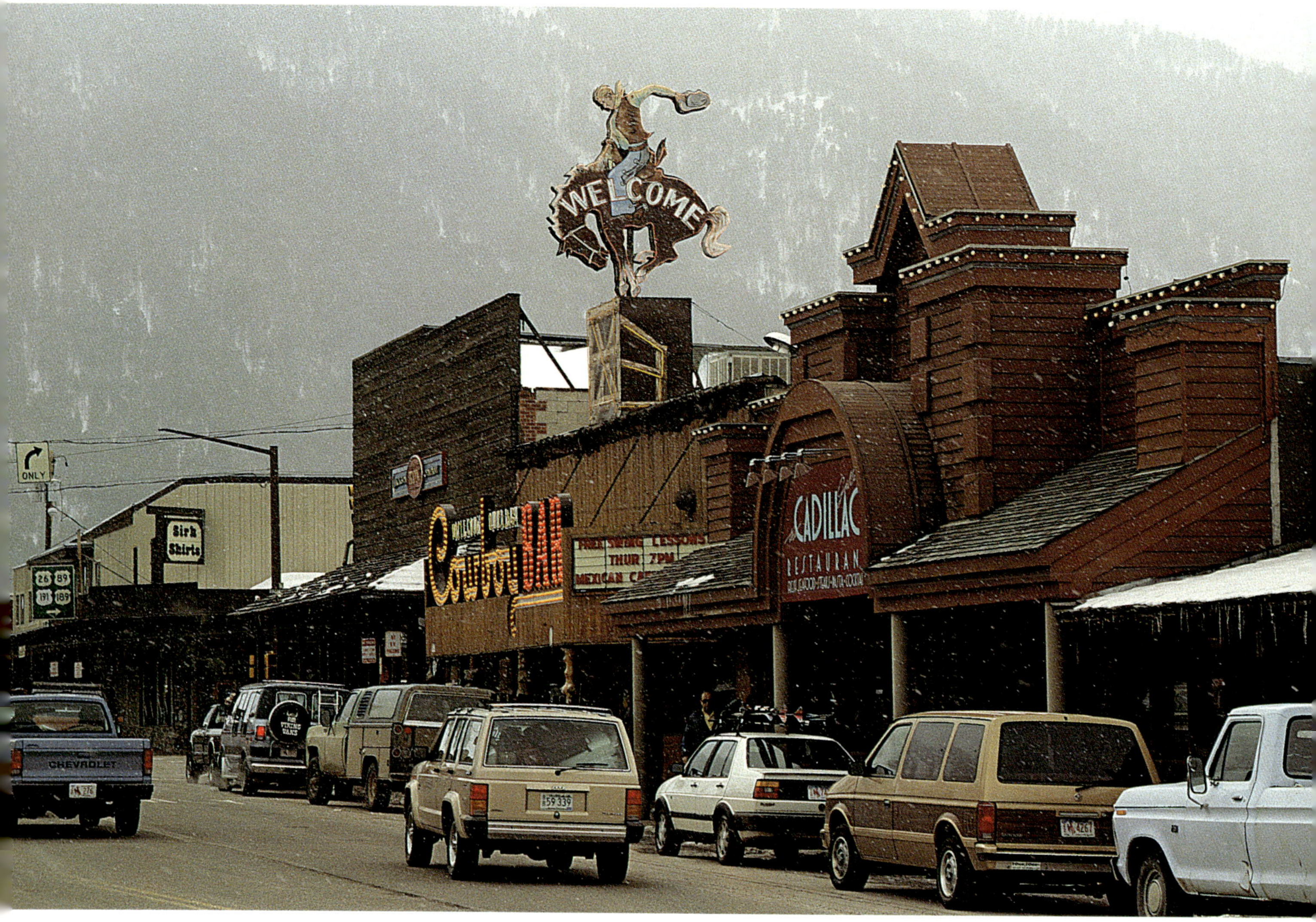

DANIEL D. LAMOREUX

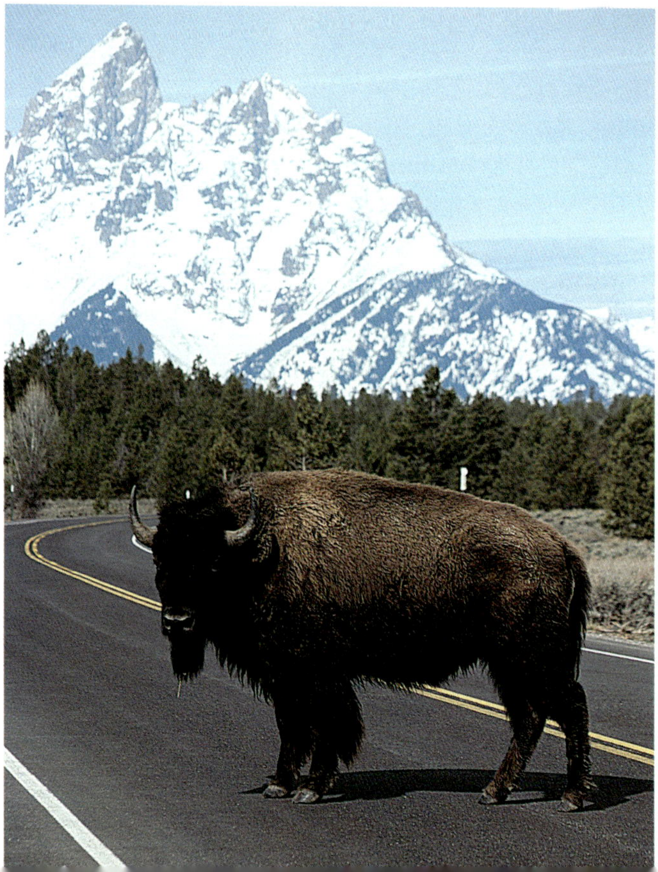

Above: Jackson's attractively quaint central business district is a steady lure to shoppers and fun-seekers.

Right: "Give me a home where the buffalo roam" is more than an old song lyric on this highway in Jackson Hole.

Facing page: Perhaps with an audience in the tram, Rob Haggart makes his mark at the Jackson Hole Ski Area.

BOB WOODALL

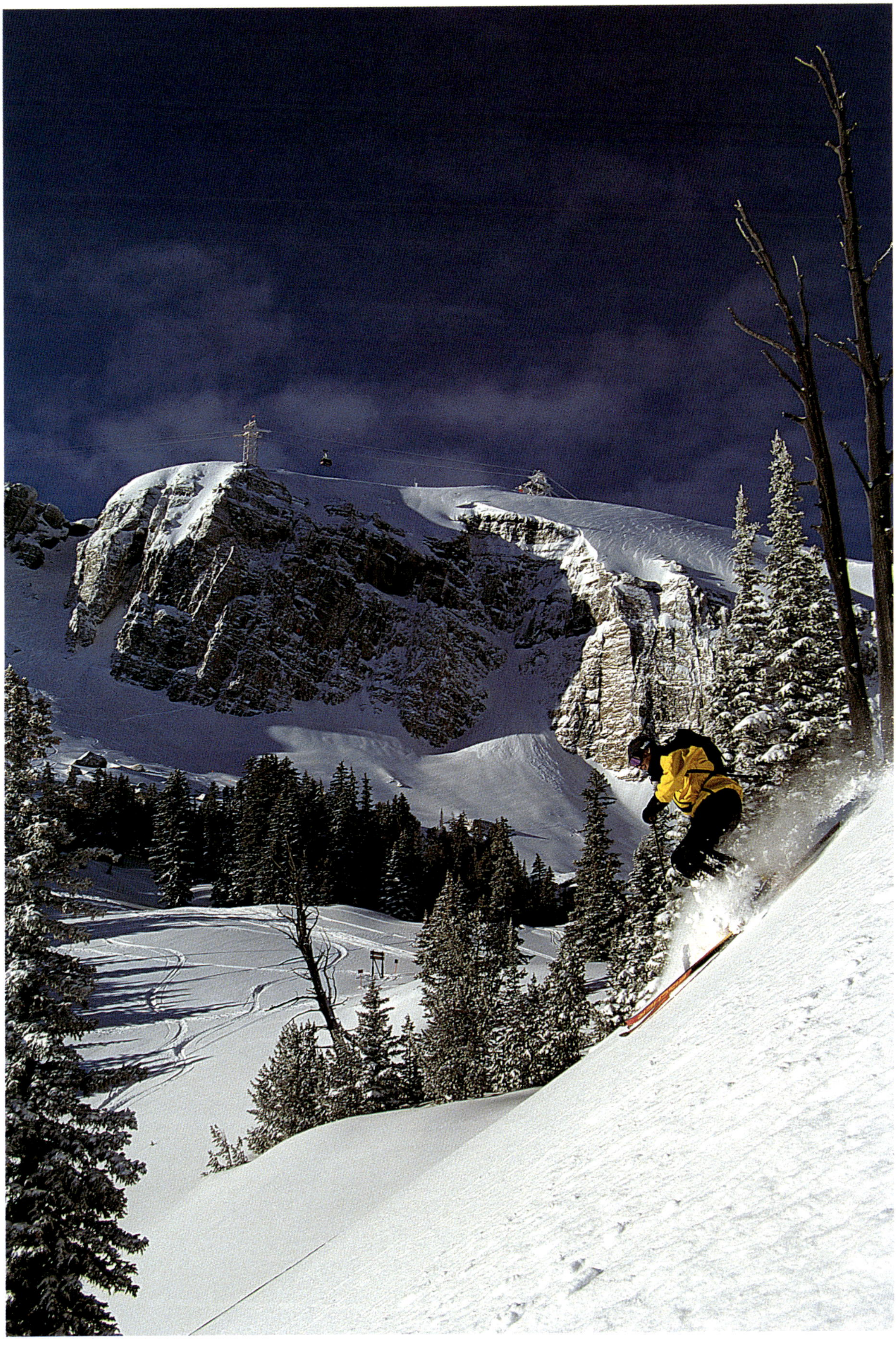

ly a family thing." In the 1990s, a rodeo child echoed his words: "All my family's ridden bulls. I'll try it this next year."

As with skiing, rodeo has fostered a sense of community as much as providing a proving ground for athletic endeavors, and as with skiing, families have kept the rodeo tradition alive in Jackson Hole. Three generations of Wheeldons have taken to the sport. After forgoing the chutes, Clark Wheeldon has watched sons Chet and Chancy, and four grandchildren–Jason, Shawn, Cody and Sadie–have their day in the arena. The line between work and play tends to disappear on a ranch, where youngsters must acquaint themselves with the antics of half-domesticated beasts unhappy with any cargo on their backs. As a result, the Wheeldon offspring growing up on the Mill Iron Ranch up Horse Creek have competed successfully in rodeos at a local and national level.

Connie and Simon Tafoya have barrel-raced and roped calves since they were youngsters, passing their love of the sport on to their four daughters who competed during the 1990s. When his son "Bucko" was only three days old, rodeo promoter Russ Moses took him to his first rodeo; by the 1990s the father-son duo were taking ribbons in their roping division at the Teton County Fair.

Rodeo continues to be part of contemporary Jackson, attracting a new generation of devotees. Today, rodeo participants include school-age girls and boys, newcomers and old-timers, and working cowboys emulating their heroes who made the National Finals Rodeo. Newcomers who heed the call of rodeo are often amazed. Jan Dalebout, a nurse, moved to the valley in 1977 from Utah and helped start the Kelly yurt park. By the 1990s, she and her husband, Paul Spillman, were taking their teen-age son, Liv, to ride bulls and younger daughter, Grace, to barrel race.

Since the 1960s, the Jackson Hole Rodeo has drawn crowds at the fairgrounds in Jackson each Wednesday and Saturday night from Memorial Day weekend through Labor Day. And if that isn't enough rodeoing for the adult cowboys, there are pickup events and practice arenas around the valley on private property and at dude ranches. For younger dudes wanting to experience being buckaroos, the summer recreational program at Teton Valley Ranch Camp near Kelly culminates with a children's rodeo.

Climbing

The Teton crags and buttresses, glaciers and canyons have been often compared to the Alps and, like their European cousins, they have been irresistible to climbers. The eons of geological and glacial movement, coupled with subsequent and steady erosion, have created what naturalist Linda Olson calls "a mountain skyline you don't find any place else in this country." The history of mountaineering in the Tetons is covered in many books and articles, including Leigh Ortenburger's 1956 classic *A Climber's Guide to the Teton Range* and issues of the magazine *American Alpine Journal.*

The 13,776-foot Grand Teton was first climbed in 1898 by William Owen and Franklin Spalding, whose names were given to the route, and local homesteaders Frank Petersen and John Shive, who were not similarly honored. Although Nathaniel Langford, the first superintendent of Yellowstone National Park, and James Stevenson claimed to have reached the summit 26 years earlier, Owen pursued recognition for the ascent until the Wyoming Legislature in 1929 gave his party the credit. Whatever the truth in that controversy, there was little activity on the Grand or elsewhere in the range between 1898 and 1930.

During the Depression years, various mountaineering clubs, including the Appalachian and Colorado clubs, began to put up routes in the Tetons. Paul Petzoldt, who would eventually organize the National Outdoor Leadership School, operated a guide service during that period. It must have been a heady time for the pioneering climbers. Geologist Fritiof Fryxell was among those leading the way, putting in a dozen new routes on peaks such as the Middle Teton, Teewinot, and Mount Owen.

Another mountaineering book, Roper and Steck's *Fifty Classic Climbs of North America*, details four spectacular and difficult routes in the Tetons: the North Ridge, the Direct Exum and the North Face routes on the Grand Teton, and the Direct South Buttress on Mount Moran. The summer of 1931, Fryxell and Robert Underhill did the first ascent of the North Ridge, an amazing accomplishment given the gear of the time. That same season Glenn Exum, who started another mountaineering school, pioneered the popular route that retains his name, jumping the airy gap at the end of "Wall Street." These days, I am happy to forgo the crux leap on the Exum Route, choosing instead to wear rock shoes and be on belay for a less theatrical crossing.

In 1936, Jack Durrance and Kenneth Henderson put in the classic Exum Direct route on the Grand, but it wasn't until 1949 that Dick Pownall, Ray Garner and Art Gilkey ascended through the rock fall of the North Face. Four years later, a party that included Ortenburger would complete the Direct South Buttress on Mount Moran. Over the next decades, summer and winter, world-class climbers joined their ranks: Willi Unsoeld, Fritz Wiessner, Fred Beckey, Yvon Chouinard, Peter Habeler, and Mugs Stump.

Climber and skier Bill Briggs' migration to Jackson Hole echoes that of other outdoorsy types before and since. The summer of 1951 Briggs first began coming to the valley to climb. "I was happy to come West and find out what the mountains were like," the East Coaster says. He remembers Jackson's one stretch of paved road–Broadway turning the corner into Cache and heading out of town. Everything else was dust.

But Briggs, like so many climbers before and since, didn't come to Jackson Hole for the cultural amenities. He hightailed it for Grand Teton National Park. After putting up routes on Baxter's Pinnacle and Symmetry Spire with Barry Corbet, Gary Hemming and Jake Breitenbach, he went to work as a guide for Exum, with whom he remained for thirty years. Even in the 1950s, plenty of budding mountaineers wanted basic and intermediate climbing classes, along with snow and ice lessons, and that demand kept Briggs and other guides on the Exum payroll. In those days, an individual guide took as many as six people up the Grand Teton, but on more technical routes, only two were secured to the leader's rope.

Although Briggs found climbing in the Tetons filled with pleasurably hard leads, he rates the first ski descent of the Grand Teton in 1971 as his most challenging adventure. Certainly, it is the feat he will be remembered for. "Everybody knew I was cra-

JAN BUTCHOFSKY

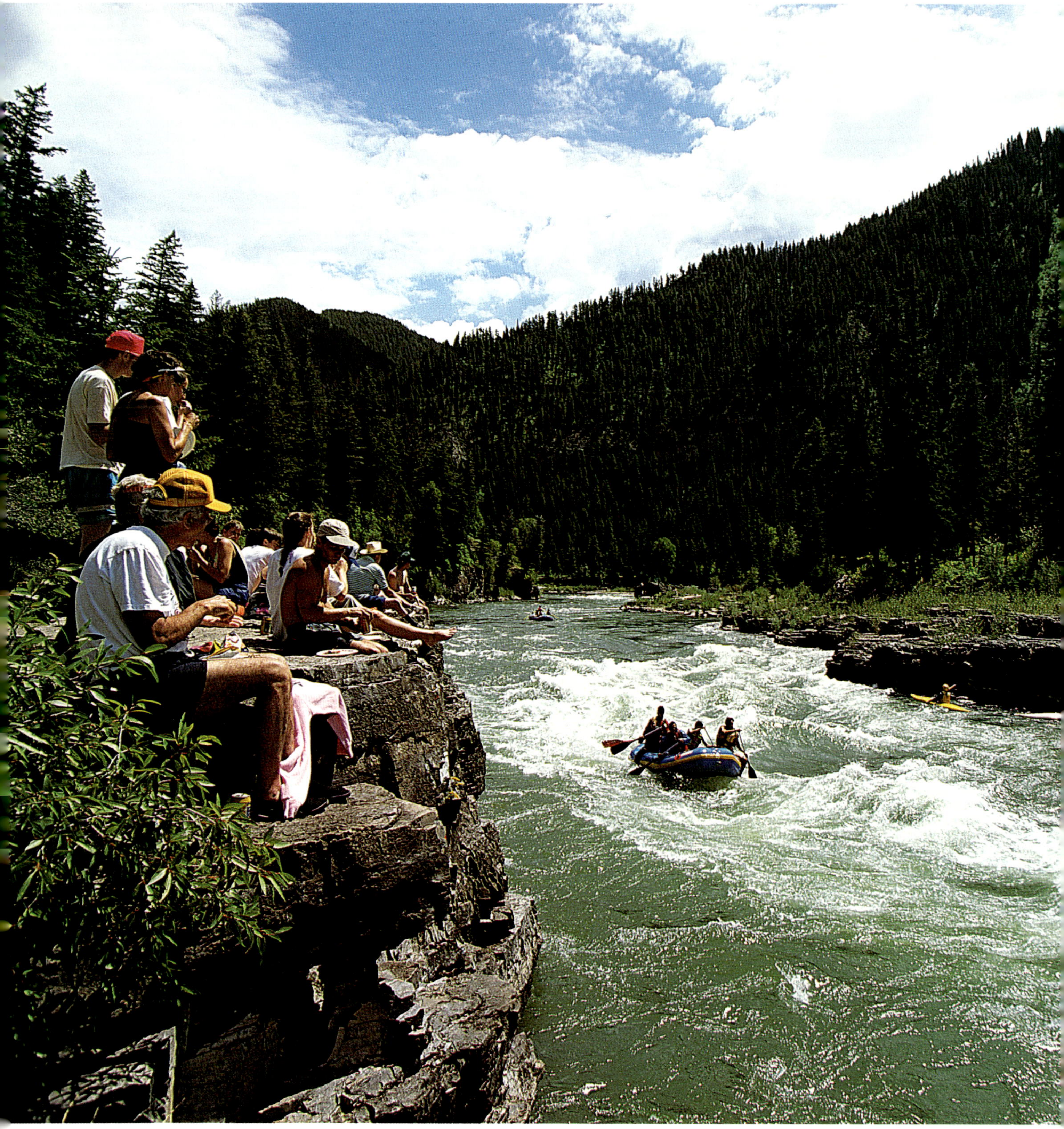

Spectators, high and dry, watch rafters and kayakers on "Lunch Counter" rapids on the Snake River.

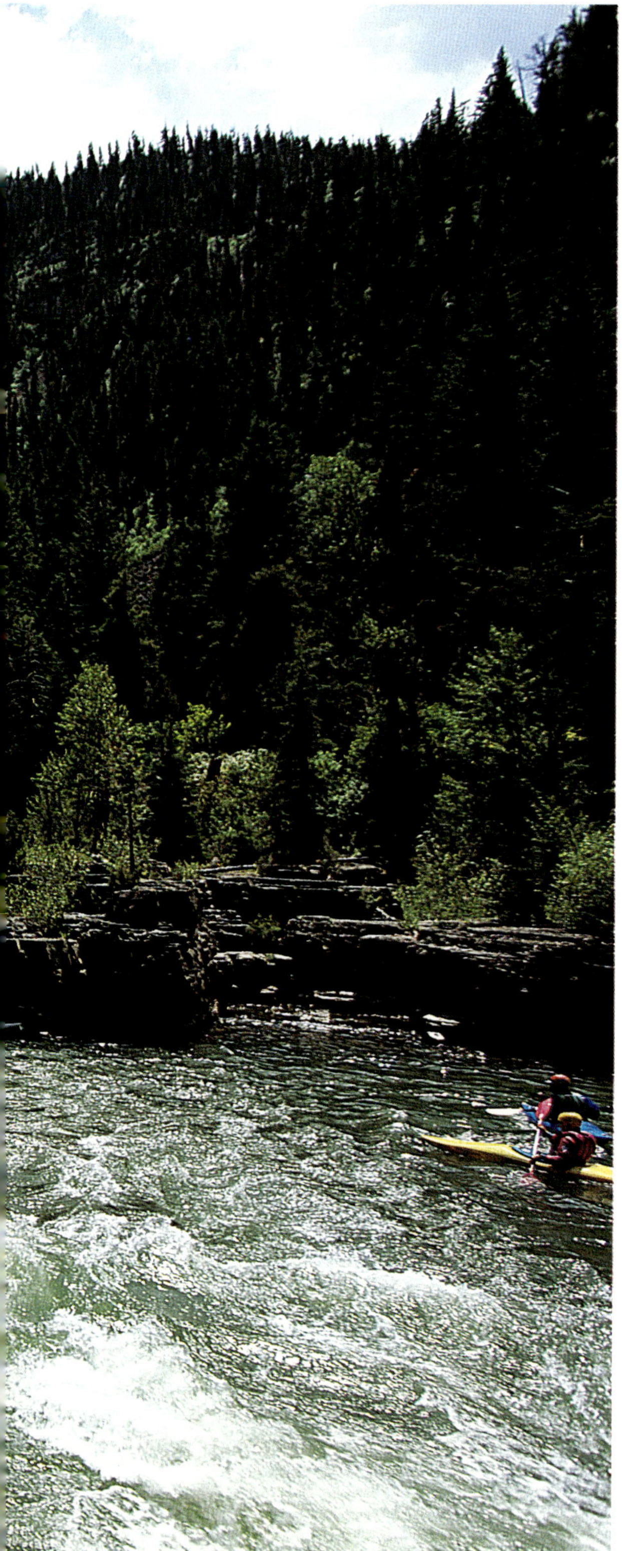

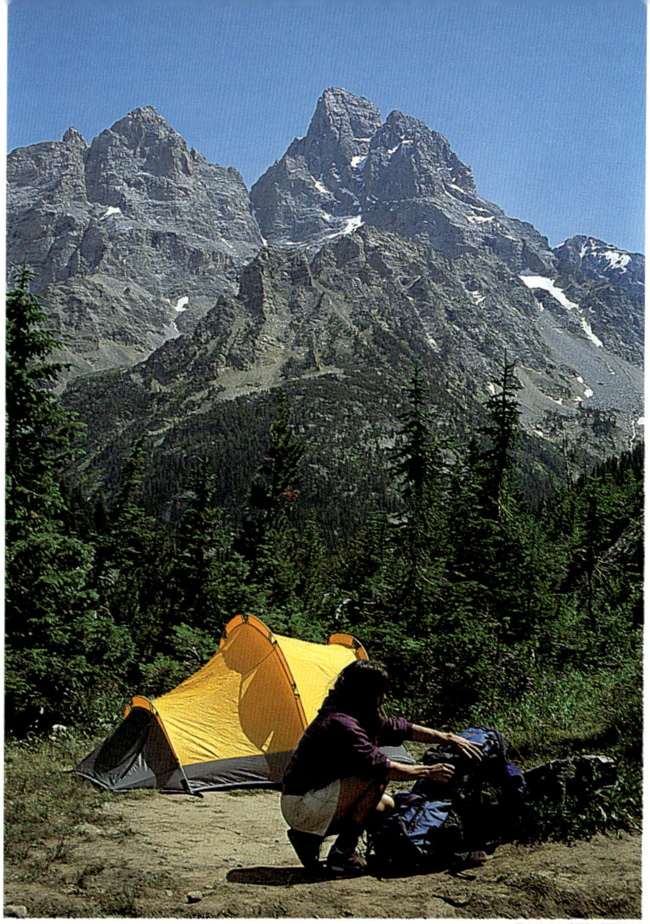

DIANA STRATTON

DAVE G. HOUSER

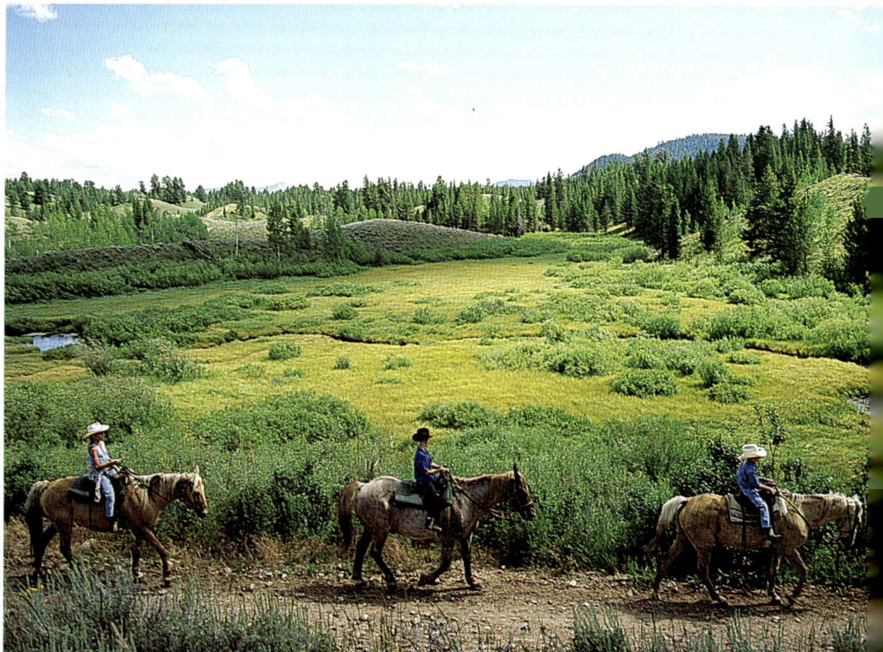

Above: A trail ride from Jackson Lake Lodge.

Top: Camping in Grand Teton National Park on the North Fork of Cascade Canyon.

zy," he says, "but I thought it was a reasonable undertaking. I was amazed that no one else could see it. The skiing was much easier than the climb."

Since Briggs' pathbreaking descent, others have found novel and exhilarating ways to get down the Grand and the other Teton peaks. A decade later, Rick Wyatt made the inaugural descent on cross-country skis, using equipment that would seem inadequate by today's telemarking standards at the Jackson Hole Ski Area or on Teton Pass. And in the 1990s, climbing guide Steven Koch made the first snowboard track on the Grand. Some, though, have eschewed the surface of Jackson Hole's mountains and buttes, preferring to leave summits, even as lowly as Snow King Mountain in Jackson, on the wings of hang-gliders and para-gliders.

Although snow and rock still beckon climbers, in recent years they have been turning to more technical sport-climbing routes. You can spot them in their brightly colored ropes and garb scaling Blacktail Butte in the Park or at Rodeo Wall just off the main highway south of Hoback Junction. And when the weather gets inclement, a sport climber's gym in Jackson allows rock jocks to hone fingers and to practice acrobatics before attending to the mountains themselves.

Water Sports

Not only skiing, rodeo and climbing have captured the valley's sporting passion. Such enthusiasm has extended from dog-sledding and snowmobiling in the winter, to fly fishing and kayaking during the summer. Presidential and plebeian golfers have practiced their swings at one of two spectacular courses–Teton Pines on the road to Teton Village or Jackson Hole Golf and Tennis at north end of Spring Gulch Road. Even if they can't stay on the green, they can take solace in the Teton views.

The lakes and streams of Jackson Hole are especially beguiling to resident and visitor. The geology and hydrology that have formed the area has created an abundance of recreational outlets. When the spring runoff comes, experienced kayakers and rafters in search of riotous whitewater head for the Snake River below the Wilson Bridge and the South Park Bridge. Later in the season, they and the commercial float trip operators move farther downstream, and navigate a series of rapids which culminate with a stretch called "Lunch Counter." Not only the Snake River entices boaters to test their skills, but also the Gros Ventre and the Hoback rivers offer similar challenges. As in the mountains, the beginner or stranger to river rafting and kayaking here would be wise to have an experienced guide.

While the roiling brown waves excite boaters, anglers anxiously watch for the rivers and streams to clear and for rising temperatures and sunny days to attract insects. Within a 200-mile radius of Jackson Hole lie some of the greatest blue-ribbon trout waters in the Lower 48–tributaries of the Snake, Madison, Yellowstone and Green rivers. Undisturbed headwaters in our mountains and the relative lack of development and dams as these rivers course through the valley mean plenty of clean Class I water for the trout.

"Jackson's kind of a neat hub to fish all of those," said Reynolds Pomeroy, guide and co-owner of Westbank Anglers. Basically, if the fishing goes sour in one spot, it's a short drive to a better locale. Although Jackson Hole has the reputation for good guides, Pomeroy said such a service is not necessary, unless the angler is looking for the normally inaccessible fishing holes. "Generally, we have good fishing in March and April, before the run-off," he explains. "Then, it doesn't get going till mid-July, but from there on, it improves daily. It fades somewhat by October."

The fishing season would not be complete without the international One Fly Contest, a by-invitation-only test of anglers' abilities to pick a single fly for the weekend's fishing. Since 1986, four-person teams having been converging on the Snake River, hoping to prove they are the best at selecting the right fly for the conditions. Pomeroy says that competitors now arrive three to four days early to practice and test their flies on the waters and trout.

Recreation Galore

Over the years, clubs have sprung up to promote events and to lobby for special interests, whether those pertain to polo and biking, running and gymnastics, Little League baseball and youth soccer. As a result, new private and public facilities, such as the Spring Creek Equestrian Center on Spring Gulch Road and the Webbs' indoor arena on Fish Creek Road, and the Recreation Center on Gill Avenue in Jackson, have gotten off the drawing boards and are open year-round. As proof of its popularity, the Rec Center on Gill Avenue attracted 128,525 people in 1995 to swim laps, sweat in the sauna, and spin down the waterslide.

With 100 programs on its schedule, the joint Jackson-Teton County Recreation Department has kept adults and children active in softball, broomball, volleyball, basketball, and more. The Rec Department maintains a dozen parks, from the Town Square to Owen-Bircher in Wilson, some with baseball diamonds and ice rinks, others with benches and picnic tables. The Teton County School District also has encouraged its students to participate in the usual team sports, as well as the ones that are typically Wyoming, such as skiing and rodeo.

But if a Jackson Holer wants solitude, she can still take a leisurely walk or horse ride along a trail in Grand Teton, or up Cache Creek, or on the Snake River levy, letting her heart race at the sight of an osprey fishing or a moose munching at a willow.

DIANA STRATTON

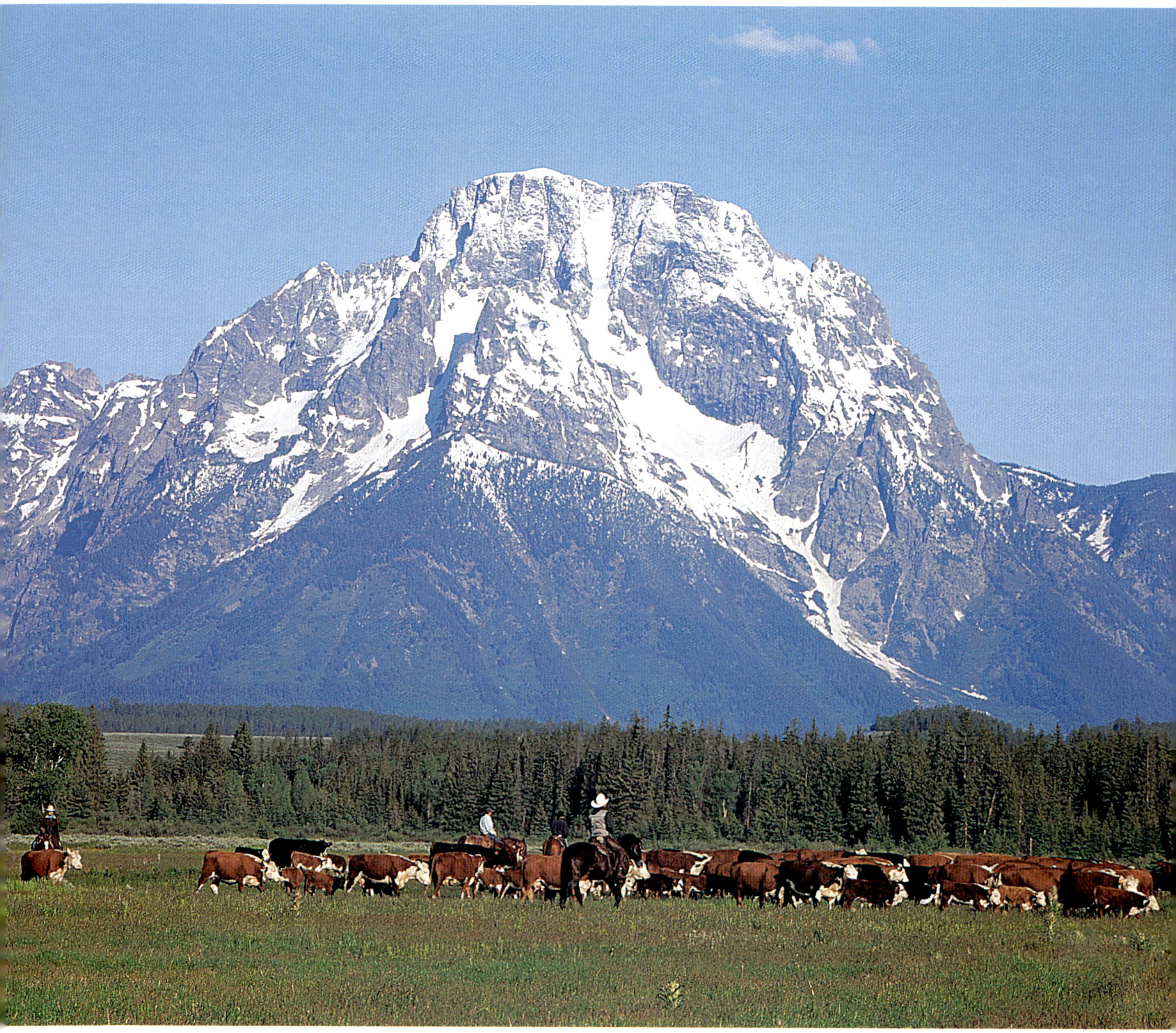

Jackson Hole cattle graze on hay and scenic splendor.

CHAPTER SIX
COW TOWN TO TOURIST TOWN

Hunters and dudes who arrived seasonally at Jackson Hole ranches in the years before World War II did not consider themselves tourists, but they blazed a bright trail for the millions of visitors who now enjoy Jackson Hole each year. Tourists, like the dudes, want to touch the wilderness and be touched by some semblance of wildness. Their coming, however, has transformed a cow town into a tourist mecca.

In 1897, a relative of the Vanderbilt family came to Jackson Hole and hired a guide to take him on a wild west safari. He was followed by other wealthy easterners and Europeans with the desire to trophy hunt for elk, moose, deer, and bear. The combination of weather and transportation costs would make guiding and dude ranching more lucrative than farming or ranching.

Louis Lovejoy opened the first ranch catering to dudes at the JY Ranch on the south end of Phelps Lake in 1908. The JY Ranch, now an in-holding in Grand Teton National Park owned by a Rockefeller family, was followed in 1912 by the spin-off Bar-BC Ranch nestled on a bench above the Snake River north of Moose and made famous in the writings of owner Struthers Burt and his son, Nathaniel. The Burts, eastern dudes before they turned to managing guests, exemplified a pattern. A wealthy easterner, following a summer of roughing it on a western ranch, riding horses, and resting from work and worry returns home and spreads the word among friends. The next summer, the friends journey west. Eventually, the dude and ranch owner disagree, the dude buys a ranch, and subsequently develops a separate clientele.

Some dude ranches evolved into the business. In 1924, Eva Sanford Topping hired on for $95 to teach school north of Spread Creek. After three years of teaching, she homesteaded the forty "pocketed" acres that became the Moose Head Ranch. According to Topping's oral history with the Teton County Historical Center, "It was all swamps and cobble rocks and willows, but it had a beautiful view." After marrying hunter and guide Fred Topping in 1927, she found herself feeding Rock Springs hunters and helping her husband build as many as forty log cabins to keep up with the demands for beds and breakfast. Once the Union Pacific Railroad advertised dude ranches, the business took off and the Moose Head's first bonafide dude arrived from

Iowa City in 1937.

Fred Herbel affectionately remembers guests from his years wrangling at the Gayleys' White Grass Ranch near the mouth of Death Canyon. When he was eighteen or nineteen, he and Monty Bassett, grandson of Granite Creek rancher Slim Bassett, were invited to chaperone five debutantes back to Pennsylvania after their summer in Wyoming; they also were invited to attend the young ladies' coming-out balls. "We drove them from White Grass to Philadelphia. The party went for a week. We stayed with the Lippincotts. There we were, two cowboys from Wyoming." Thirty years later, Herbel is still grinning.

Almost a dozen guest ranches, including the Triangle X, Lost Creek, and Trail Creek Ranch, are scattered from Buffalo Valley in the north to Wilson in the southwest. They, like their predecessors, see families return year after year. While some of the operations have changed little since the 1930s and 1940s, others have transformed themselves to suit the contemporary dude. For instance, the low-ceilinged main cabin of Becky and Roy Chambers' Flying V Ranch east of Kelly has been replaced by a sizable lodge and new cabins in the revamped Gros Ventre River Ranch.

But the dudes only bolstered the valley's summer economy. Employment and business opportunities continued to dry up the other three seasons. Native son Roger Millward's words succinctly portray the long off-season: "If it wasn't for the local grocers, people would have starved." In *The Cocktail Hour in Jackson Hole*, Donald Hough paints a more humorous portrait of what the valley's residents did to keep themselves alive and entertained, which included the consumption of prodigious amounts of alcohol.

People also seemed to have spent an inordinate time, before and after World War II, entertaining themselves at illegal gambling tables, roulette wheels, and slot machines. When JoAnne Byrd first came to the valley in 1944, she worked a summer at The Wort, which was at the heart of Jackson Hole gambling. She was an innocent sixteen-year-old, the world was a little crazy, and World War II appeared nearing an end. "There was a feeling of celebration that hasn't existed since. You always danced until morning. The bankrolls were this big," she said, curving her fingers into a wide C. "You just can't believe the money. And the fights...just wild."

Clarene Law, who was born in Rexburg, Idaho, recalls going into The Wort as a child with her parents: "I never have seen as much money." Byrd says she has heard two stories about the demise of gambling. The first, that a Salt Lake City photographer had taken pictures of the gaming tables and people playing them; the valley's residents became frightened by the exposure. The second, that Governor Milward Simpson closed it down when he took office in 1955. Whatever the reason, gambling became another memory in Jackson Hole.

Success Stories

Although people had tried to stimulate interest in Jackson's winters since the 1930s, two decades later Georgie Morgan and Virginia Huidekoper, co-founders of the *Jackson Hole News*, designed a brochure to entice tourists to come for skiing and for the elk refuge sleigh ride. "It was the same old thing," says Morgan, who moved here in 1949 from New York City. "We needed some winter business. Everybody was on elk and crackers for the winter."

The Jackson Hole Chamber of Commerce, formed in 1946, had only 90 members as late as 1976. Then-president Bob LaLonde successfully urged the chamber to hire its first director, Ralph McMillan. Although McMillan is remembered best for his annual hairstyle changes, within two years he had gained 600 members for the chamber. At the beginning of its fiftieth year, the chamber boasted 875 businesses, with 141 of those in merchandising, 143 in lodging, and 61 in food service.

Motel and restaurant owner Clarene Law was named Jackson's Citizen of the Year by the Chamber of Commerce in 1974 and three years later she was honored as Wyoming's Small Business Person of the Year. Law moved to Jackson in 1959 with experience as a reporter, secretary, and clerk. Within a few years, she bought the Antler Motel, added 48 rooms, and operated the Topper Restaurant and Gulf Station.

Now, Law's family corporation, Elk Country Motel Incorporated, has torn down the gas station, leased out the restaurant, and built the 49'er Inn Motel. Law devotes time to civic clubs, cultural organizations, and politics, and ran successfully for the Wyoming Legislature in 1990. Law recalls the less hectic days of the 1960s, when people would sit and talk on the log fence in front of the Antler. "We called that the 'spit and whittle days'," she said. "But [then] we continued to grow." The old adage about what makes a business successful applies as much to Law's holdings as it does to all of Jackson Hole: "Location. Location. Location."

The Jackson Hole Ski Area may have triggered the valley's current economic boom. In 1963, the Jackson Hole Ski Corporation found enough federal low-interest loans to get construction underway at Teton Village. The corporation's major partners, Paul McCollister, Alex Morley, and Gordon Graham, guided development of the Jackson Hole Ski Area, which opened in 1965. The following season, an aerial tram was put on line, lifting skiers 4,139 feet to the top of Rendezvous Bowl and the beginning of a 4.7-mile run. During the summer, the tram operates to provide non-skiers spectacular views of the Tetons and the valley.

Skiers visiting the area did not increase as dramatically as they had at other Rocky Mountain resorts. In its third year of operation, Jackson Hole Ski Area registered 59,000 skiers. Bad snow years hurt skiing and sales of property at Teton Village. Even in 1975, skier numbers increased only to 89,100. However, when airlines added direct flights from Chicago and Texas, skier numbers started moving upward, from 187,200 in 1985 to 246,600 in 1988, a substantial one-year increase. Although 1991 was the banner year, with approximately 273,000 skiers, the 1995-96 season approached that number, according to the Forest Service which monitors the Ski Area's usage.

Ultimately, the establishment of the Ski Area at Teton Village changed the valley's demographics and land values. By extension, it created more jobs, and "an abundance of opportunity" for entrepreneurial types, as local economy watcher Jonathan Schechter said. The increase in summer and winter visitors–whether coming in by automobile or on one of the several daily jet flights from Salt Lake City and Denver–

WILLIAM J. THOMPSON

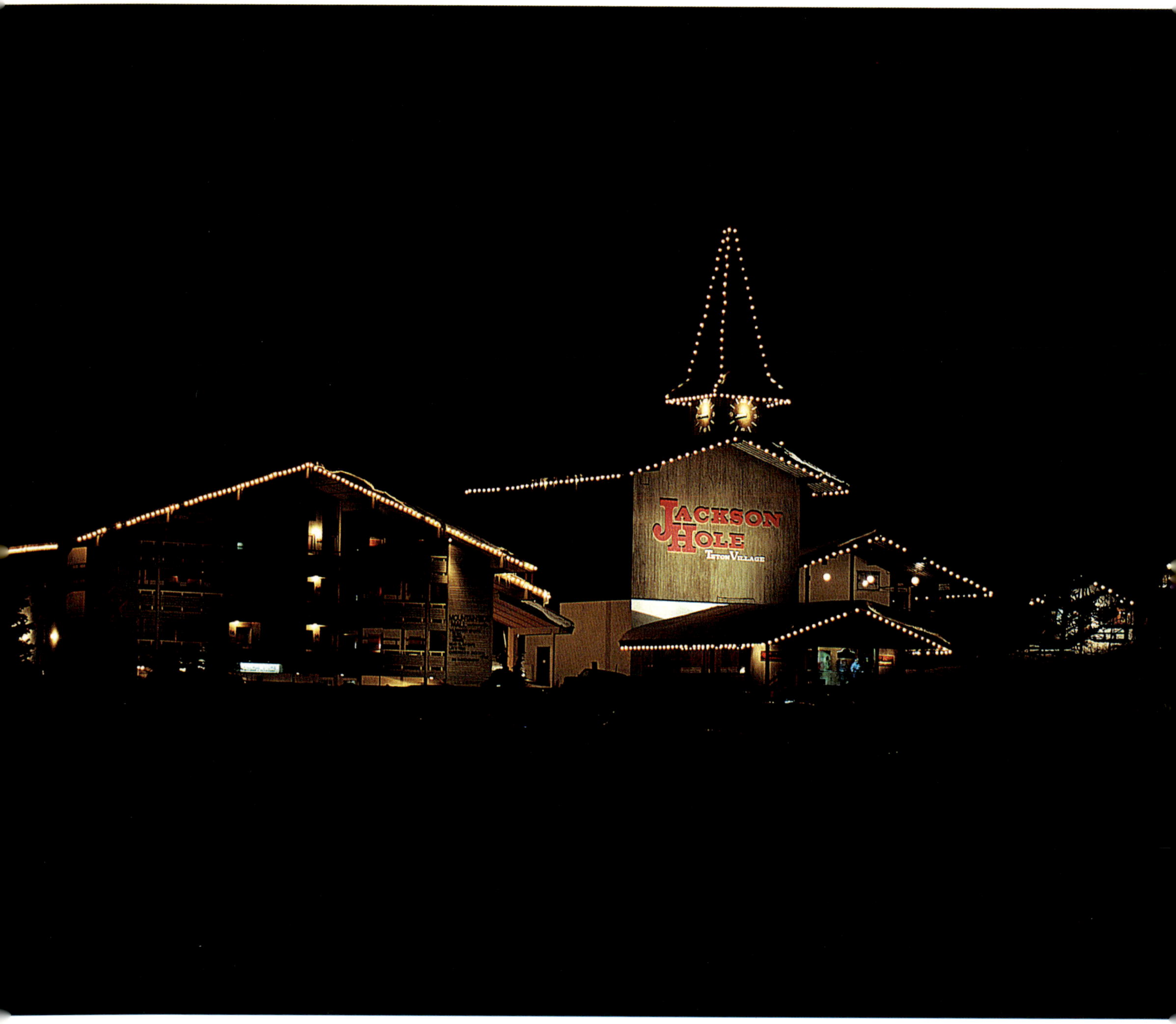

Teton Village Ski Resort takes on a magic-kingdom look at night.

JAMES BLANK

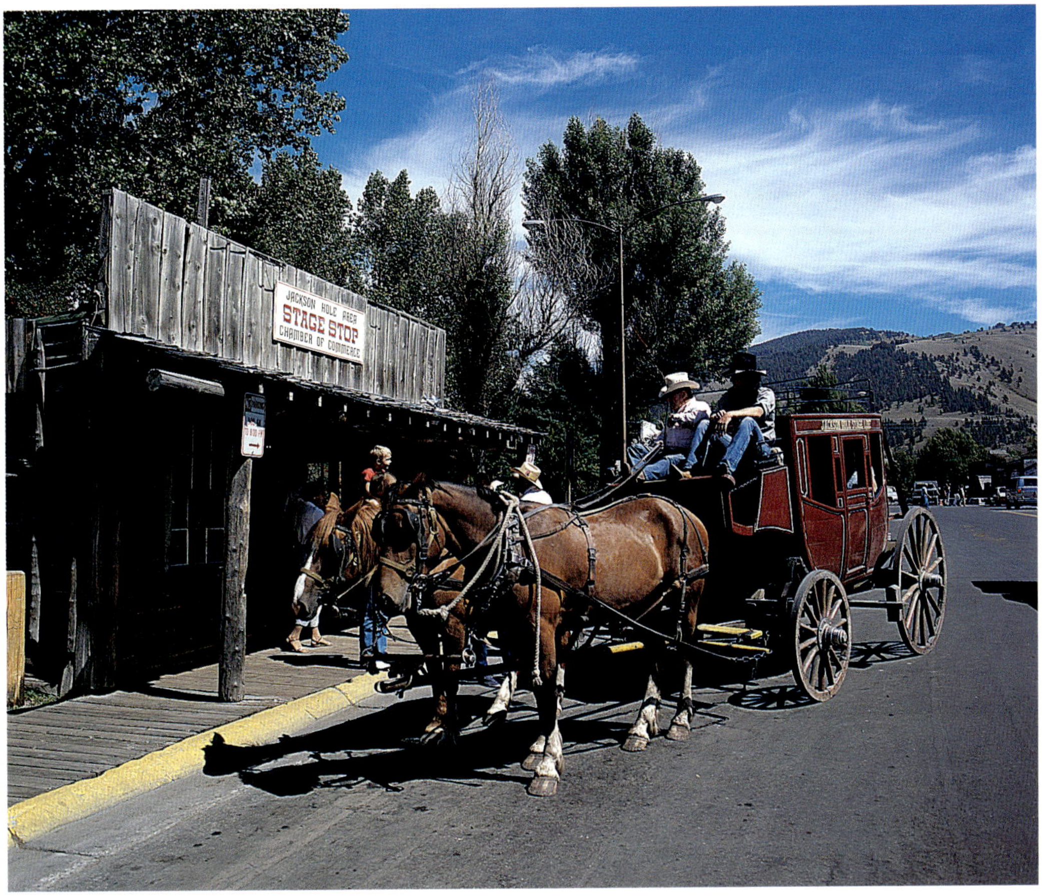

A stagecoach ride now is simply fun, not the vital form of transportation it was once in the West.

DAVE HOUSER

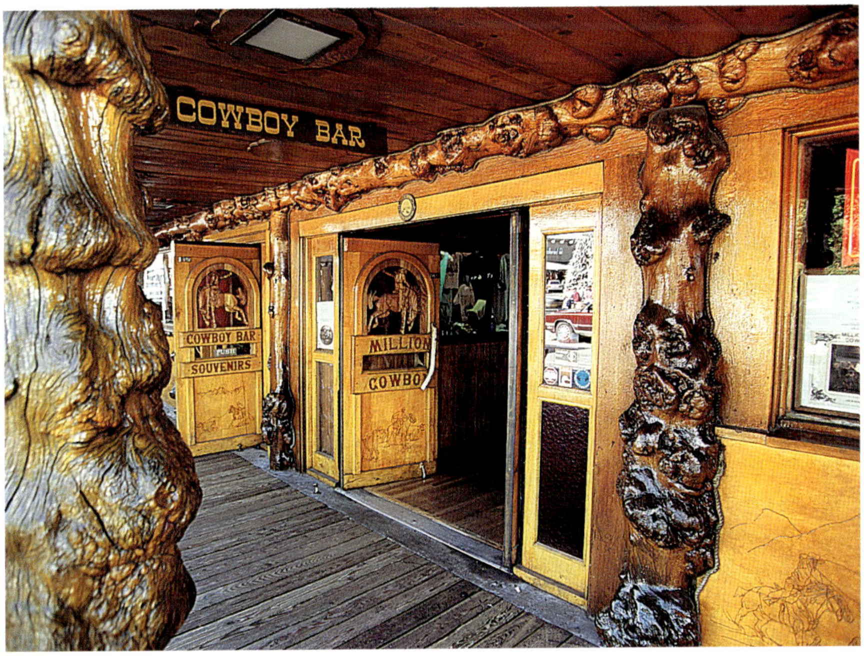

The Million Dollar Cowboy Bar in Jackson.

is paralleled by an increase in sales tax revenues for town and county. The rest of the state, which has yet to experience similar growth, looks on enviously. As the joke goes, "There's Wyoming and there's Jackson Hole," meaning this valley might as well be another state.

According to Schechter's calculations, between 1981 and 1991, Jackson Hole was the only area in Wyoming to see increased taxable sales. While Teton County showed a 4.2 percent growth in taxable sales, the other twenty-two counties combined experienced a decline in sales by an average of 5.2 percent. That also means that Teton County's cost of living is the highest in Wyoming.

Some long for the good old days, when restaurants closed their doors and motels took down the vacancy signs. There is a bumper sticker that reads *Bring Back Off Season.* Previously, when April or September came, folks took off for warmer climes and play time. Now, too many people in Jackson Hole, as elsewhere, have mortgages to pay and family and business commitments to keep.

Coming and Going and Coming Back

One person described Jackson as a place where people traditionally have come and gone, and that seems true for the oldtimer and the newcomer.

Bob Nethercott was born in 1914 in a "little cabin" on present-day Nethercott Lane in Wilson, where his grandfather had homesteaded in 1895. However, his father, barber Robert Silas Nethercott, had "a bug to travel. We went all up and down the [Pacific] Coast." Bob returned to Jackson Hole in 1932 after graduating from high school in Vallejo, California.

After graduating from high school in 1966, Jennifer Lucas went to college and traveled for ten months in Europe, singing with "Up With People." Eventually, she earned an accounting degree from the University of Wyoming. Although she worked for eight years outside her native valley, Jennifer planned her vacations to coincide with trailing the family's cattle up the Gros Ventre. She finally returned in 1979 and opened an accounting business.

Sandy Shuptrine made it to Wyoming in 1966, working a season for the Jackson Lake Lodge Company. When she flew out of the valley at the end of the summer, she felt distressed to be leaving the place. Then, in 1971, while her husband, Dick, was still flying in Vietnam, she drove with then-toddler Shannon to Jackson and put down their life-savings on a house. Within two years–after working for Powderhorn Mountaineering, driving bus, and volunteering day care–they decided to buy White Glove Cleaning Service.

From day one, both of the Shuptrines, like Clarene Law, were involved with the community, sitting on an advisory committee for the planning commission and joining the League of Women Voters. "I was thinking of it as my home," Sandy says, "and seeing things that needed participation. You can make positive things happen if you participate." To that end, she ran successfully for the county commission as an independent in 1991.

Knowles Smith's story of settling in Jackson Hole will sound familiar. He visited

Jackson Hole in 1969, and despite the threat of a scalping on the Town Square, he came back each summer over the course of five years. "We were outcast," he says. "No matter what you looked like or how you dressed, you were an outsider. You were considered a hippie."

Smith stayed away the two years he worked as a beekeeper in upstate New York, before returning in 1976 and meeting his wife, Barbara, who was baking at Bru's Buns and Breads, now The Bunnery. They decided to settle elsewhere in the West, but a year later, they were back in Jackson Hole.

In 1980, when Suzanne Young started flipping hamburgers at Camp Creek Inn up the Hoback Canyon, she thought she was between jobs. By 1985, Young was director of the Chamber of Commerce, a post she held for six years. During her tenure, she helped usher in the era of direct flights from Chicago and Texas, and a lodging tax used to promote winter vacations in Jackson Hole. These days she consults with everybody–from arts groups to the airport board, from ski hill areas to a cleaning company–admittedly helping them to deal with problems created by her success at advertising the valley.

Linda Olson has spent all of her twenty-five years with the National Park Service in Grand Teton National Park. While a student at the University of Illinois, she did summer field work here in 1969 and came back for good in 1971 as a naturalist. "I met and fell in love with a ranger type," she says with her usual directness. Her husband, Jim, initially worked as a climbing ranger–he claims first ascents in the Tetons on his extracurricular vita–but now keeps the Park's computers on line.

Scores of ski bums, whether they came in the 1930s or the 1970s, have stayed after the snowy season, learned a trade, started families, moved into their own homes, raised a Lab or two, joined committees, were appointed to public and private boards, and put their names on the ballot. Like the Shuptrines, many of these folks decided living in Jackson Hole "wasn't going to work if we did not own our own business." Among the successful businesses begun by newcomer acquaintances and friends–whether they arrived in the 1940s or the 1980s–I can count a general store, an espresso shop/bakery, two accounting firms, and several restaurants, building contractors, and ski shops. Those who did not have entrepreneurial instincts left for a few years and came back as teachers, hospital social workers, massage therapists, and attorneys.

Building Community

Near the beginning of *A Pattern Language*, Christopher Alexander states: "Individuals have no effective voice in any community of more than 5000 to 10,000 persons." Old-timers and newcomers occasionally find themselves agreeing with that statement. There is a sense that the explosive growth witnessed in Teton County, especially in the last five years, means changes to the way we deal with each other and the land, and it means a loss of community. Countering that sometimes negative outlook is the hope that we have learned a lesson from communities that have not weathered demographic evolutions as well, that here, as Frank Craighead puts it, we have "a chance to do it right."

Sandy Shuptrine defines community as "a place where you belong, where there is a

HEIDI DAVIS

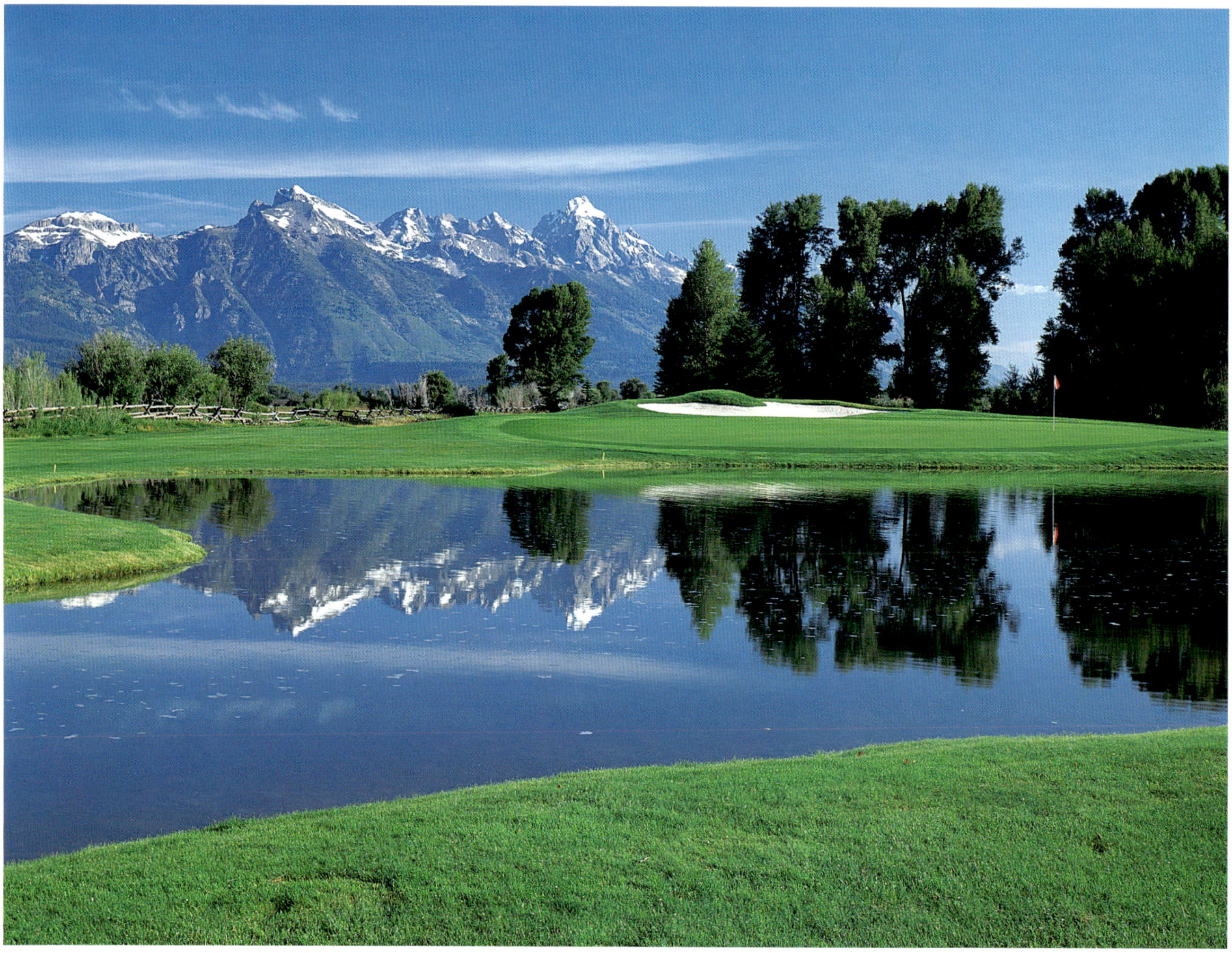

Above: How well can you concentrate on the little white ball at Jackson Hole Golf and Tennis?

Right: Jenny Lake Lodge in the park.

Facing page: The Teton Range, mirrored in Jackson Lake.

GLENN VAN NIMWEGEN

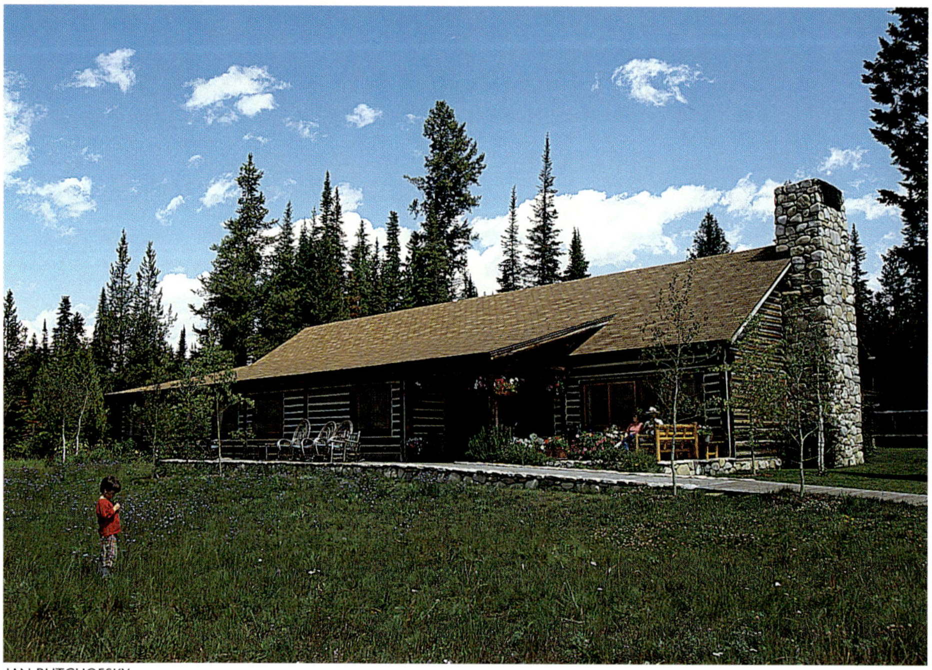

JAN BUTCHOFSKY

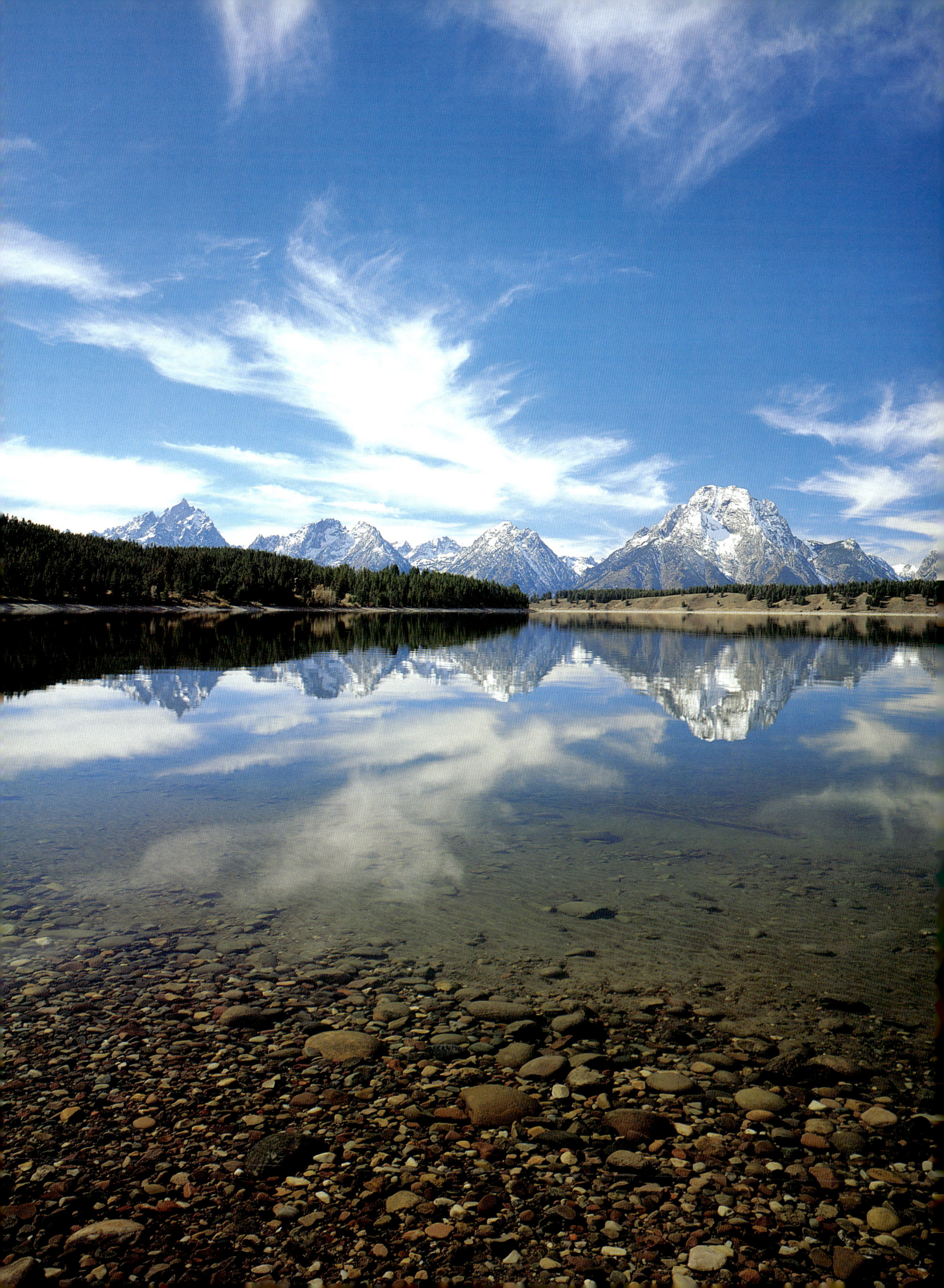

certain mutual respect among individuals. People support each other, have fun, socialize, join together to provide for the common good, such as schools and libraries and day care. They do things that demonstrate their commitment to each other and to create a healthy environment."

As early as 1985, Suzanne Young says, people were afraid Jackson was going to be a town you would not want to live in, a town with bad signs and bad zoning. But in 1989-90 people vocalized their concerns when told by the county's Planning Department that as many as 60,000 people could be living in Jackson Hole–if every piece of land that was zoned for residences were built on. With the permanent population now approaching 17,000, residents wonder about the effects of a population three and a half times greater. How will the projected 60,000 residents affect traffic, the economy, and the quality of life for human beings and wildlife, and residents' ability to retain an "effective voice?" Teton County's comprehensive plan, adopted in 1978, was revised in 1994 in response to those questions and concerns. The 1994 plan, which was adopted after many public hearings and meetings, continues to be applauded and cursed for its restrictions.

The Economy

Economy watcher Schechter uses the metaphor of "a landlocked island" to define the economy of Jackson Hole. "We don't have the luxury of having a lot of extra resources to bail us out," he says. A resort community depends on a predictable flow of visitors, visitors who can be tourists driving through the town of Jackson en route to Grand Teton or Yellowstone national parks or second-home owners living here for two weeks each year.

A handful of cottage industries have somewhat lessened the valley's dependence on tourism and related industries: motels and bed-and-breakfasts, restaurants, retail outlets, and hunting and recreation outfitters. Several have marketed their products nationally and internationally. The umbilical cord for the glasses of skiers, boaters and astronauts, Croakies, had its birth here. Although Life-Link's manufacturing plant moved to Bozeman, Montana in 1988, research and development continues in Jackson, and the company has expanded its line to include backcountry snow shovels and poles.

Frannie Huff, granddaughter of pioneer doctor C.W. Huff, has been manufacturing outdoor clothing for adults and children since 1981 when she re-tooled Wyoming Woolens. Because of the high cost of living in Jackson, Huff relocated her manufacturing plants and seconds outlets to Afton and Cokeville, Wyoming; there, because of the lower cost of living, she has found a more stable, less expensive work force. Between those operations and a retail outlet in Jackson and one in Park City, Utah, Wyoming Woolens employs 120 people.

Despite the light industry inroads, the economy still relies on visitors, even when those visitors eventually decide to root themselves in Wyoming. During the late 1980s, a second-home market mushroomed. It was a different phenomenon than what had occurred in the early 1970s with condominiums; that market, as well as real estate in general, slumped between 1981 and 1986.

Development Pain and Gain

Even as late as 1989, there was a perception that the "economy was not going great guns," but then came a new demographic and economic trend. Large homes had been built previously, even as palatial as 20,000 square feet, but they were rarities. With the 1990s, architects and contractors were asked regularly for designs and construction of large, expensive homes, from 6,000 square feet to 15,000 square feet. The houses began appearing on Fall Creek Road and along the Gros Ventre and Snake rivers.

There was a big difference between this wave of second- and third-home migrants and the one that signaled speculation in the condo market during the 1970s: These home-buyers stayed in the valley for more than week. Some–because of the communication revolution, the enticing lack of a state income tax, and regular, daily air flights–even transplanted their businesses to Teton County. "They discovered you didn't have to ski to live here," said Roger Millward. Initially, the flood of new homes benefited contractors and their subs, such as excavators, plumbers, and electricians. But the benefits trickled down to furniture and household providers, to retailers, and to grocers.

The second-home owners' allegiances continue to be a little divided, according to Shuptrine, but "by the same token, they have contributed to the community," sitting on non-profit boards and contributing to their financial well-being. "We've become a wealthier community," Schechter said. The influx of people with cash and demands has "lifted the whole economy. Maybe overlifted it."

To deal with real estate costs, a growing number of people commute over Teton Pass from Teton Valley, Idaho or up the Snake River Canyon from Afton, Wyoming making those outlying towns the bedroom for Jackson. The non-profit Jackson Hole Community Housing Trust, organized in 1990, has built thirty-six Mountain View homes on South Park Loop Road. It hopes to have twelve more houses on property at the bottom of Snow King. But the Housing Trust has only brushed the surface of the problem, a problem that resort communities in the Rockies are facing. At least another sixty people are waiting for the Housing Trust to purchase additional property, providing them with the chance to be homeowners.

Efforts to preserve ranch land, including the Hardeman ranch near Wilson, and the Spring Gulch ranches west of Jackson, are being made by groups like the Land Trust. It must be remembered that some of the original impulse to establish a national park in Jackson Hole was embodied by a desire to save cattle ranching as a way of life. According to Marshall Gingery, since 1929, there have been several moves to include Spring Gulch in the park or in the Elk Refuge.

While 192 acres of the Hardeman ranch property, which parallels the highway between the Snake River and Wilson, have been preserved through contributions to the Land Trust, the Spring Gulch Preserve is seeking to protect all or part of 5,000 acres in Spring Gulch, property estimated to have a value for between $60 million and $100 million. Four ranches–owned by Rod and Joyce Lucas, Phil and Betty Lucas,

JAMES BLANK

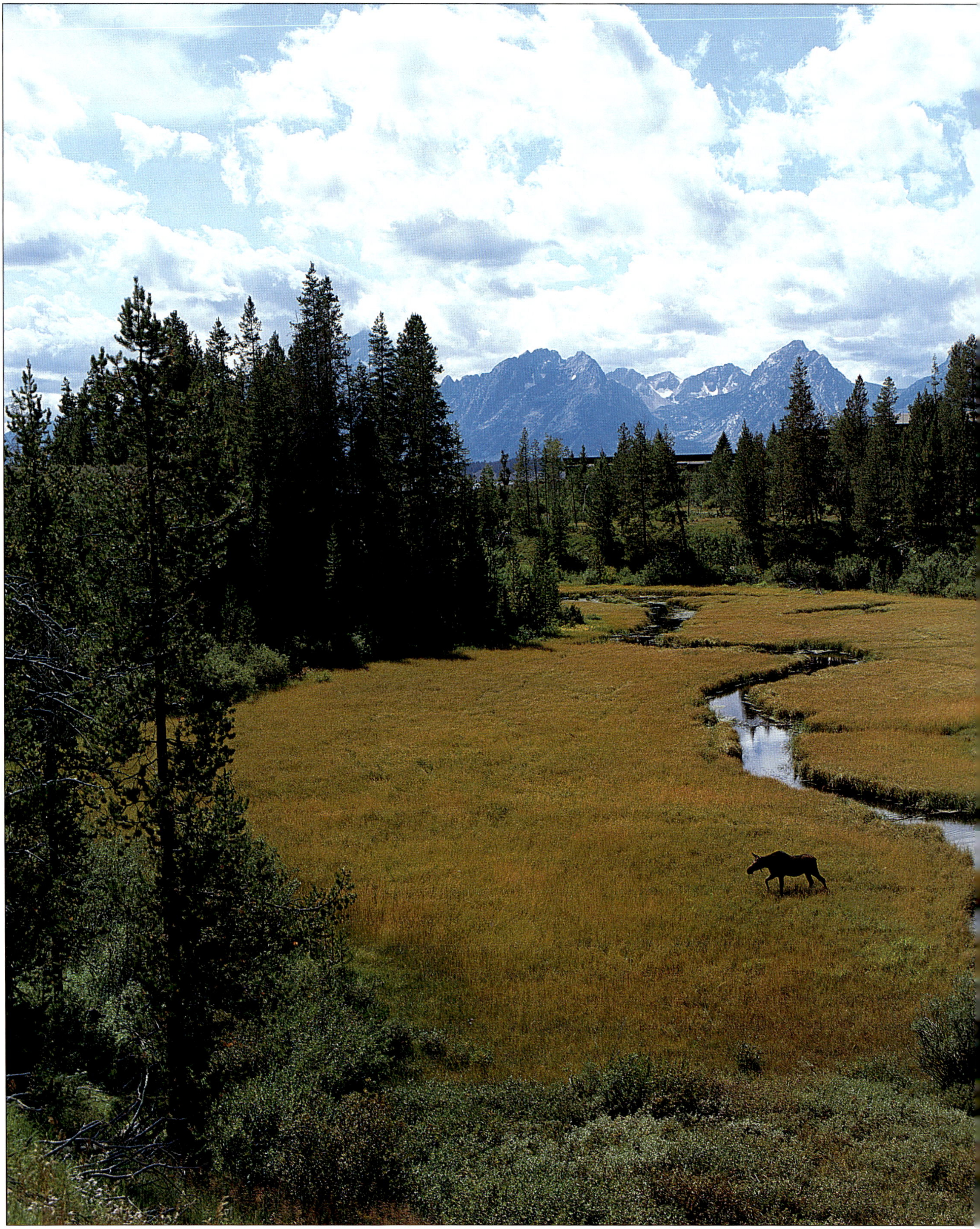

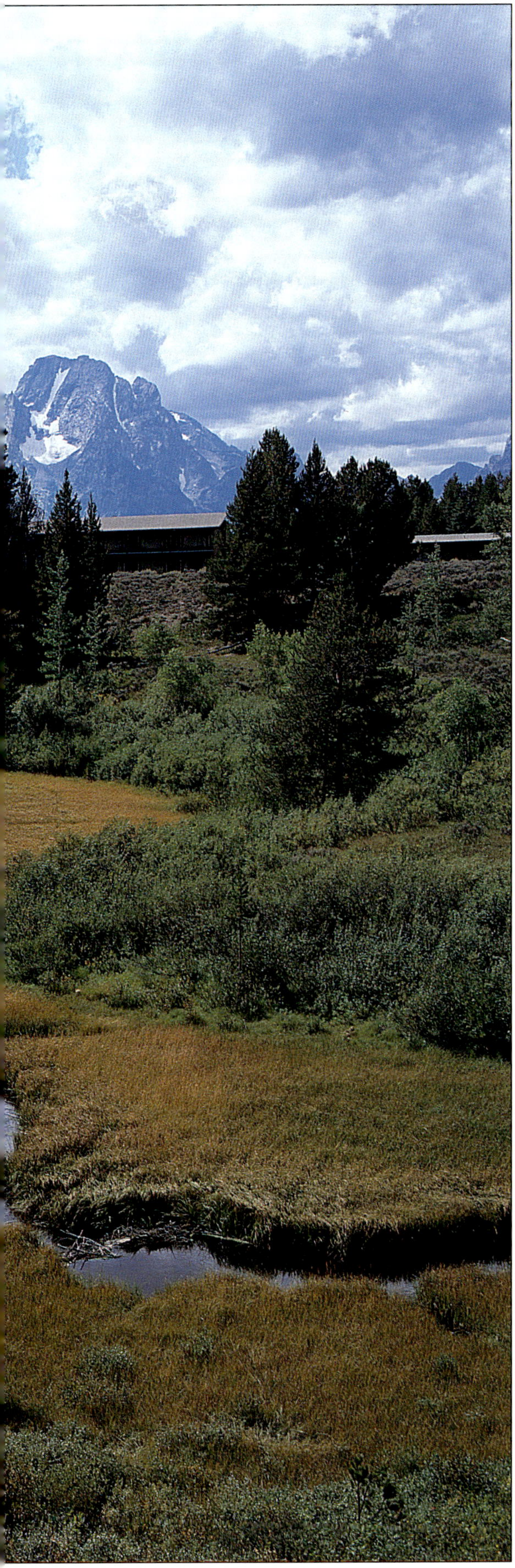

WADE MCKOY

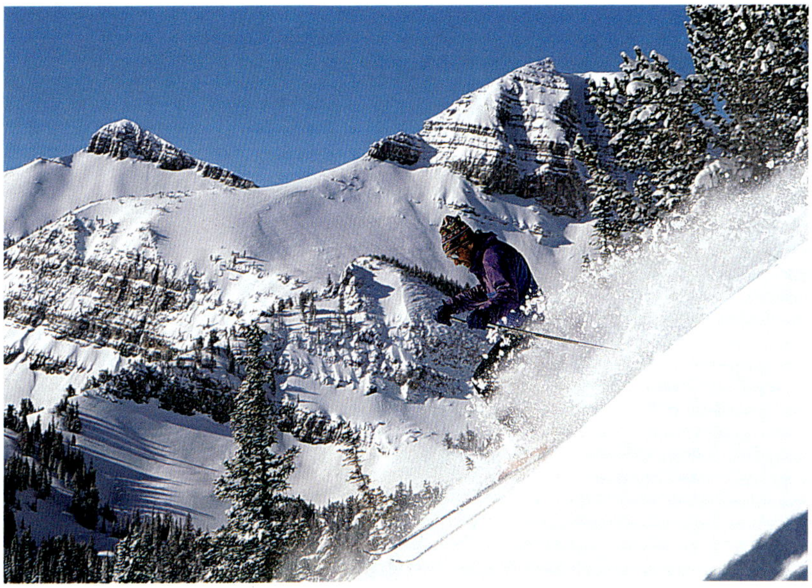

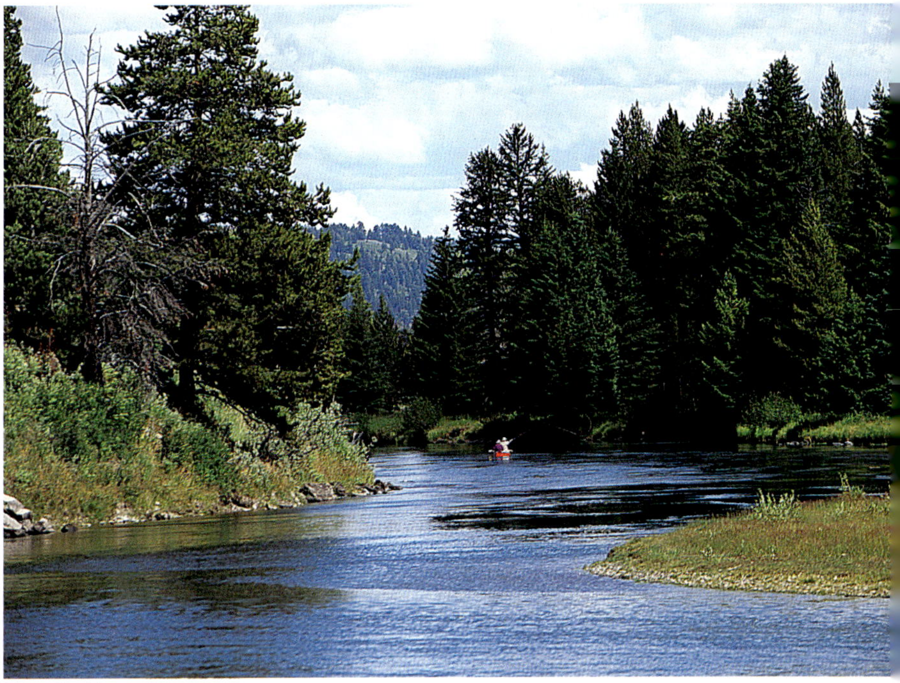

JAN BUTCHOFSKY

Above: Placid boat-fishing may be a far cry from whitewater thrills, but the Snake River accommodates them both.

Top: Expert skiers from around the world find everything they want on the slopes at Jackson Hole.

Left: Moose on the move in Grand Teton National Park.

Clifford and Martha Hansen, and their daughter, Mary Mead–are targeted by the preservation effort. Clifford Hansen is a former Wyoming governor and U.S. senator. Gingery stresses the western heritage value of ranch lands as reason to advocate the Preserve. "They are just as important as the open space and wildlife," he says. "Twenty years from now wouldn't it be nice, if there was this open space for walking or biking There are spring creeks and there are cultural resources. People could see a ranch house and see all that goes with ranching."

For years on Togwotee Pass, a sign beckoned the visitor: *Howdy Pardner Yonder Is Jackson Hole, The Best of the Old West.* The friendly advertisement with its cartoonish cowboy has been replaced by less rustic signs near Jackson's city limits. With or without such homely encouragement, people will find Jackson Hole.

HENRY H. HOLDSWORTH

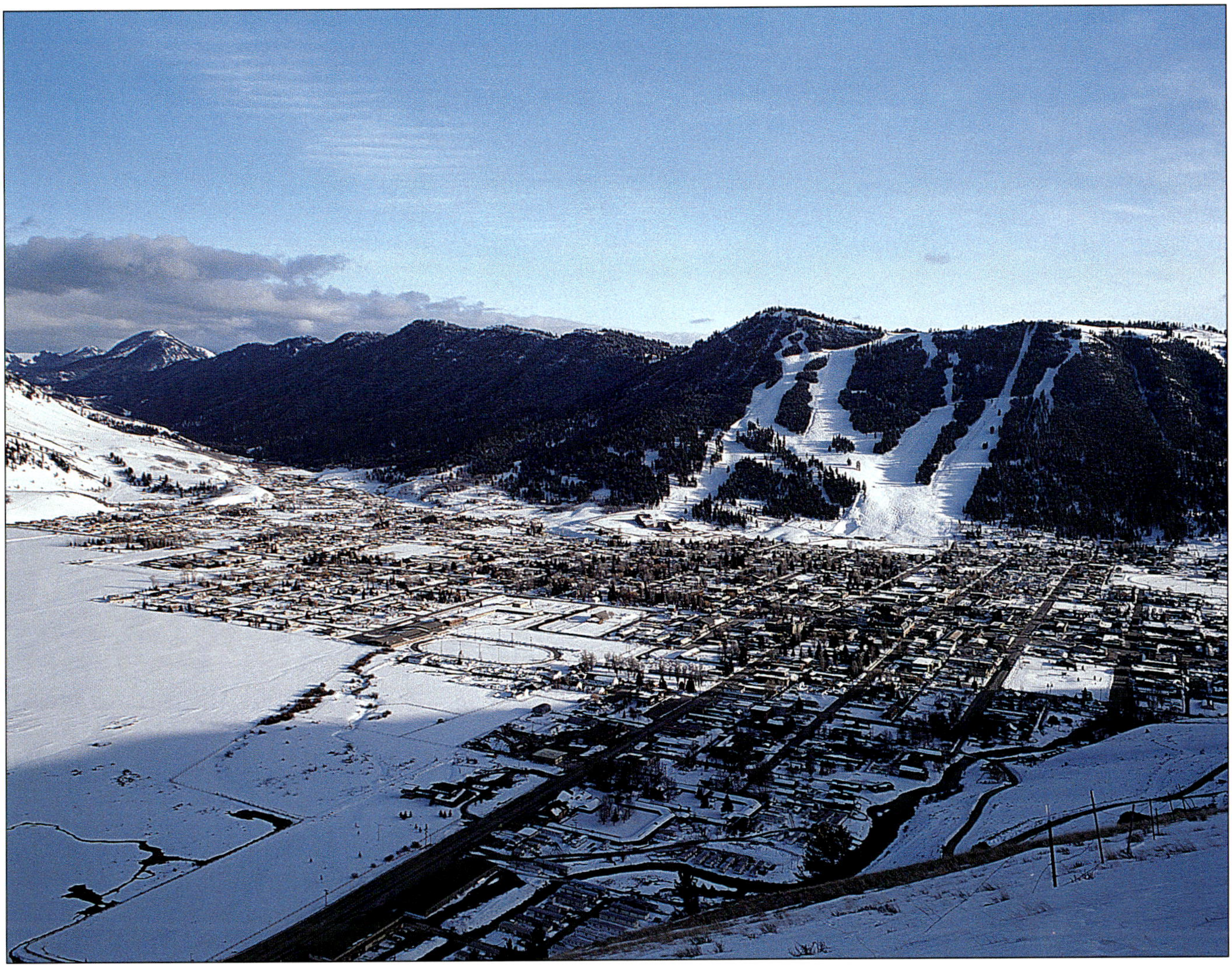

DAVE G. HOUSER

Above: Wintertime once was the off-season in Jackson. That changed with the arrival of world class ski resorts.

Right: Elk-viewing sleigh rides keep the National Elk Refuge busy in winter.

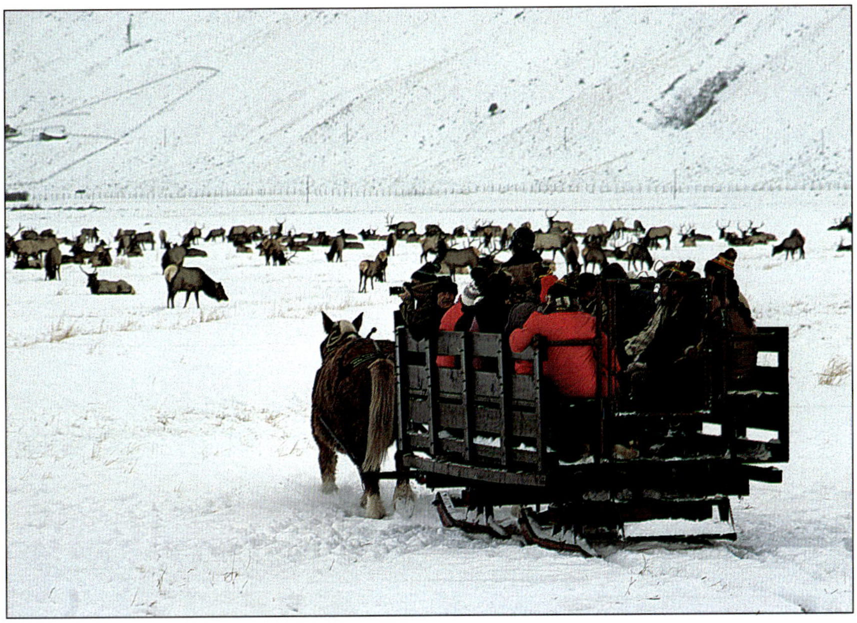

CALENDAR HIGHLIGHTS

JANUARY

Jackson Hole Powder 8's
Telemark Powder 8's
Noble Franzen Memorial Cutter Races
Forty-Niner Ball

FEBRUARY

Shriners' All-American Cutter Races
Moose Chase Cross Country Ski Race
Grand National Powder 8's
Jackson Hole Theatre Company production
Cowboy Ski Challenge

MARCH

Town Downhill
Annual Celebrity Ski Extravaganza
Jackson Hole Theatre Company production
Annual World Championship Snowmobile Hillclimb

APRIL

Pole-Pedal-Paddle (triathlon event)

MAY

Elk Antler Auction

Memorial Day Weekend: Jackson Hole Open Tennis Tournament
(USTA sanctioned) at Teton Pines
Memorial Day Weekend: Old West Days and Rendezvous

JUNE

Annual Eastern Idaho Old Iron Auto Rally
Annual Rendezvous Pro Am Golf Tournament
Spring Fling

JULY

Dancers' Workshop Arts on the Hill Summer Dance Festival
Old Fashioned Fourth of July Festival
Fourth of July 10K
Jackson Hole Writers Conference
Mountain Artists Rendezvous
Grand Teton Music Festival
Annual Wilson Chicken Fry
Teton County Fair
Snow King Hill Climb

AUGUST

Grand Teton Music Festival
Annual Hoback Picnic
Mountain Artists Rendezvous
Annual Culinary Arts Exhibition

SEPTEMBER

Jackson Hole One Fly Contest
Annual Moran Picnic
Moose Chase Marathon
Jackson Hole Wildlife Film Festival
Jackson Hole Dance Festival
Jackson Hole Fall Arts Festival
Old Fossils Tennis Tournament (USTA sanctioned) at Teton Pines
Annual Arts for the Parks Awards Ceremony
LOTOJA—210 mile bike ride from Logan, Utah to Teton Village
Rendezvous Mountain Bike Race

OCTOBER

Jackson Hole Fall Arts Festival
Annual Fall Pro Am Golf Tournament (Teton Pines)
Quilting in the Tetons

NOVEMBER

Ski Ball
Annual Town Lighting Celebration

DECEMBER

Annual Christmas Bazaar
New Year's Eve Torchlight Parades

For information on dates, contact the Chamber of Commerce, 307-733-3316

Overleaf: Cow and calf moose at Oxbow Bend of the Snake River. HENRY H. HOLDSWORTH

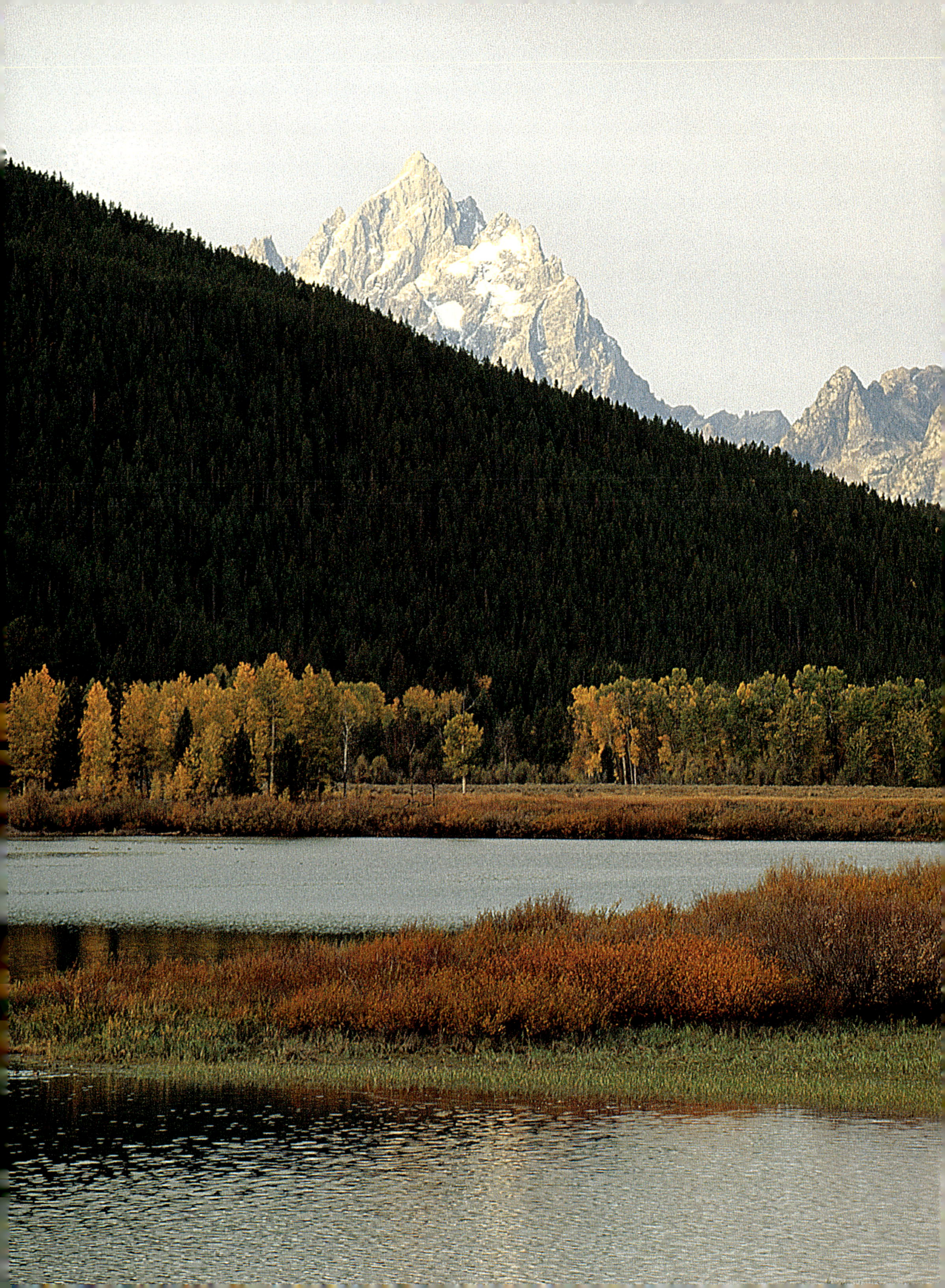

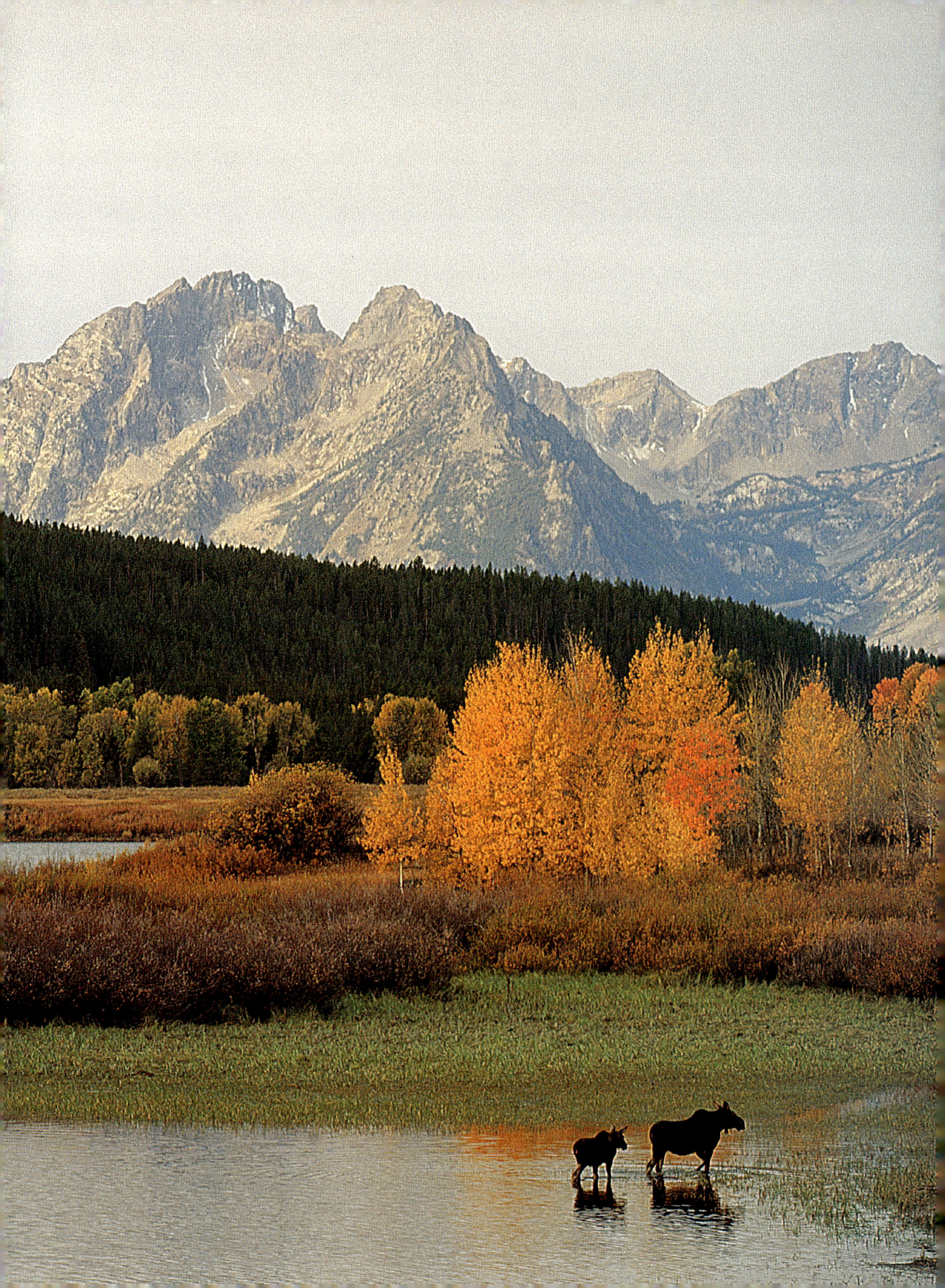

INDEX

Italics indicate photographs

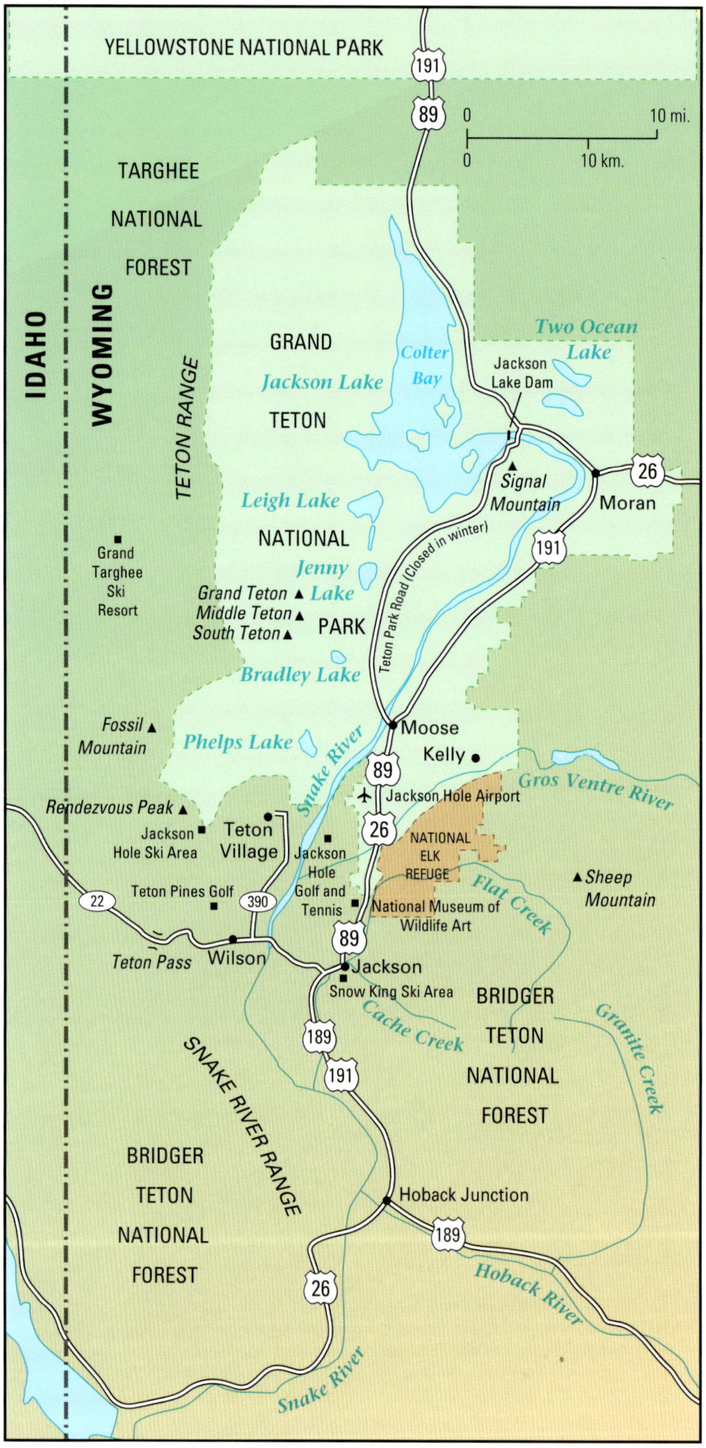

PATRICIA ISAACS, PARROT GRAPHICS

ACKNOWLEDGMENTS

I want to thank the women in my writers group who took time from busy schedules to read and criticize this as a work-in-progress: Kirsten Corbett, Geneen Marie Haugen, Susan Marsh, Sidney Smith, and Tina Welling. I also want to thank Valley Bookstore owner, Steve Ashley, whose comments were helpful. I want to acknowledge the Teton County Historical Center, the Teton County Library, and the Jackson Hole Chamber of Commerce, and the people who work in them for their assistance. I also want to thank American & World Geographic Publishing editors Barbara Fifer and Bill Hanson for their direction and confidence.

Most of all, I want to acknowledge the people in this valley who shared with me some portion of their stories. Thank you for that honor.